THE BASIC PRINCIPLES

D1051071

THE BASIC PRINCIPLES OF PEOPLE ANALYTICS

Written by:
ERIK VAN VULPEN

With a Foreword by:
DAVID GREEN

Published by:
WWW.ANALYTICSINHR.COM

This edition first published November 2016
ISBN: 978-1-5411-4839-0

© Analytics in HR B.V.

Written by Erik van Vulpen (erik@AnalyticsinHR.com)
Editing by Nando Steenhuis
Cover and image design by Nando Steenhuis
Correction by Jet Krantz and Joanna Bankersingh

Special thanks to David Green for writing the foreword and providing valuable
input and feedback.

All rights reserved. No part of this publication may be reproduced and/or copied
without the express written permission of the publisher.
Contact the publisher at info@AnalyticsinHR.com.

TABLE OF CONTENTS

FOREWORD

The Head of People Analytics – let's call him Alexander - was working late. His company, one of the largest technology businesses in the world, had provisionally settled on the multi-million dollar location of its key new operation in China.

Alexander was curious. He had the workforce plans that told him the number and skills of the employees that would be needed by his company when the new site opened. He also had the projections of additional employees that would be required as the site grew in its first three years.

Then Alexander compared his organisation's plans with the external talent supply and demand data he had asked his team to collect for the provisional location in China. It didn't take him long to identify the problem. Not only were there not enough skilled potential employees in this geography, but the few that were there were in high demand from the companies that were already established in this particular city.

Alexander saw immediately that his company was about to make a very expensive mistake; one that could potentially cost it millions of dollars and prevent it from achieving the growth projected from the new site. He turned to the talent supply and demand data for the other cities in China that had been under consideration.

After finding more favourable locations from a talent perspective, Alexander worked with his analytics counterparts across the rest of the organisation. Together they soon had a new and better set of recommendations for their board to act upon.

Alexander is part of a new and growing area of HR called 'People Analytics'. Like Alexander, these pioneers seek to drive better, faster and more accurate business decisions through the use of data and analytics. Studies by the likes of Bersin by Deloitte find that companies that have successfully adopted people analytics enjoy better talent outcomes and better financial performance than their peers.

People Analytics is one of the most talked about areas of human resources. Articles in the trade press and social media abound, analysts predict it will become a core component of human resources and conferences devoted to the topic are sprouting up all over the globe. However, the number of organisations adopting people analytics is only rising slowly.

Why? Partly, this is because many human resource professionals are confused about people analytics and don't know where to start. Many of the skills required to do analytics have not historically been present in HR. Much of the literature available on people analytics is too theoretical and can confuse, rather than help, HR professionals seeking guidance.

In this book, Erik van Vulpen has successfully demystified people analytics. In doing so, he has provided a practical guide for those looking to get their people analytics programs started as well as those looking to accelerate to the next level. This book is ideal for those looking to move beyond static reporting and generate not only improved business outcomes but also help make work better for their fellow employees.

Across the book's ten chapters you will learn what people analytics is together with a brief history, why it is increasing in popularity, the different maturity levels and the skills and capabilities required to practice analytics in HR. Erik also walks you through the people analytics process: how to ask the right questions (of the business), selecting, cleaning and then analysing data as well as the critical components of interpreting and communicating the results and effecting change.

I am confident that after finishing this book, the reader will be more knowledgeable, more confident and feel emboldened to grasp the opportunity offered by people analytics. Enjoy the book and good luck with your people analytics journeys.

David Green

1.

PEOPLE ANALYTICS

Business case

Google is one of the most innovative companies in the world. After being founded, they experienced astronomical growth. The company expanded to more than 20 000 employees in ten years' time, more than doubling their population every single year. In 2007, the amount of new hires peaked; 200 new employees every week.

This meant that Google had to spend a tremendous amount of time on recruiting and selecting new employees. Every new applicant was interviewed by the hiring manager and by their future colleagues. Some managers spent half their week talking to new hires!

Since Google invested an extraordinary amount of time on these interviews, they decided to run the numbers to measure their effectiveness. A small task force of Google data scientists analyzed the predictions that interviewers made about a candidate's future performance. The task force compared these predictions to the actual performance of new hires in an effort to find out how accurately the interviewers could predict performance. The findings were surprising...

What is people analytics?

People analytics is about looking into these numbers. Instead of (or in addition to) relying on gut feeling, people analytics helps organizations to rely on data – just like it helped Google evaluate their hiring process. This data helps to make better decisions. By running the data, decisions can be made based on facts and numbers: people analytics is a fact-based approach to managing people.

As the example shows, Google thought their managers hired world-class performers. However, this was an assumption they had never tested before. That is quite 'un-Google-y'. Instead of relying on gut feeling, the head of Human Resources (HR) decided to crunch the numbers to see how effective the interview process really was – and how it could be improved. Even small improvements would make a big difference because employees spend so much time interviewing new candidates. These improvements are what people analytics is also about. By adopting a fact-based approach organizations are able to validate their assumptions on how best to manage people.

People analytics is about analyzing organizations' people problems. Human Resource professionals have long been amassing valuable HR data. Yet despite the value it holds, this data has hardly been used at all. When organizations begin to use this data to analyze their people problems and to evaluate their people policies by connecting them to business outcomes, they will start to engage in people analytics.

Since people analytics involves aggregating and analyzing data, it requires a skill set that goes beyond those considered 'traditional' to HR. People analytics is a combination of Human Resource Management (HRM), finance and data analytics.

People analytics is the combination of HRM, data analytics and finance.

Skills needed for people analytics

People analytics is an overlap of HRM, finance and data analytics. This means that organizations need varied skillsets in order to implement analytics. This involves more 'traditional' knowledge such as recruitment, hiring, firing and compensation. Insight in these HR processes will help to make sense of the data that is required to run the analysis, but will also help to make sense of the outcomes of the analysis.

Organizations are beginning to realize that a solid understanding of HR practices is not enough. It is also necessary to analyze the data. This requires a firm foundation in statistic and data analytic techniques. In the example, Google analyzed whether interviews predicted future performance. This can be measured by correlating the data, running a regression analysis, performing structural equation modeling, or by using one of the many other ways to analyze the data. Some of these techniques work considerably better than others. The knowledge required to choose the best way of analyzing the data goes beyond the traditional HR practitioner's skillset. We will talk more about these different data analysis techniques in chapter nine.

In order to perform data analysis, you need data. This data often originates from different systems. For instance, to perform their analysis, Google had to ask their interviewers to rate candidates as well as collect data from their Applicant Tracking System and their Performance Review System. Thus, people analytics often involves aggregating data from different sources or systems; this aggregation requires programming skills as well as knowledge of the company's IT infrastructure. To analyze the data, you need an analyst with an aptitude for working with data and statistics.

Lastly, it is important to communicate effectively with the business. This is key at the start of analytics, but also when you interpret results. As we will discuss later, it is also important to begin with an analytics question that is important to the business. In addition, when the data analyst relays his/her findings, it is vital to interpret and communicate these results.

This can be a challenge because the numbers sometimes contradict the manager's or HR practitioner's gut feeling. Transforming the results from 'analytical numbers' to actionable data visualizations is an often forgotten part of analytics. Furthermore, the way you communicate the data influences its impact. You can present the data in a meeting, display it in a dashboard or send it in an email. Different ways of communication require different ways of visualizing the data. This capacity to effectively communicate the data is very important for the successful implementation of analytics.

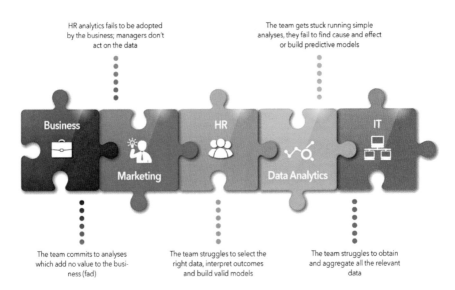

People analytics consists of a combination of different skillsets, some of which are rarely found in HR.

In summary, people analytics goes beyond the skillset that is traditionally present in the HR department. The unique combination of skillsets needed for analytics also makes it challenging to develop an organization's analytical capabilities. In order to develop these competences, HR should look for new hires with different skillsets or work together with departments in the organization that has these skills in abundance (e.g. Finance and IT). In chapter five we will talk more extensively about the skills needed in an effective analytics team – and what will happen when your team lacks certain skills.

Why is people analytics so important?
When you say analytics, most people think of finance or marketing. These are fields that already measure everything they can measure. Every sale is registered, on their website every button click is recorded and every conversion is measured. In fact, a well-oiled Finance Department is able to show the conversions for every single dollar spent on online marketing.

However, HR has never done this…

…which is strange, because people are oftentimes a company's most *valuable* and most *expensive* asset. In general, companies spend around 70% of their budget on personnel expenses. This number is even higher for service firms and other companies with many highly educated employees. It is peculiar that organizations have almost no data about how effective people-spending really is, even though it constitutes the majority of the organization's expenditure. Insight into how these expenses contribute to the organization's effectiveness is vital for its existence and its competitive edge. This is where analytics comes in. It is a tool to measure the efficiency, effectiveness and impact of people policies and spending.

As written in our Google example, measuring the effectiveness of people policies is important and can have far reaching consequences on how the business is run.

Around the turn of the new millennium, new research showed that interviews did not predict future performance very well. Indeed, when interviews were not done well they were a very unreliable tool for selecting new candidates. It turned out that this also held true for Google.

Candidates who came to Google for a job talk never had a second chance of making a good first impression. By the first hand shake, the interviewer subconsciously knew whether he liked or disliked the candidate. The interviewer would then spend the next hour looking for cues that would confirm his/her first impression. It turned out that when a candidate made a bad first impression it was almost impossible to turn this bad first impression into a good second impression.

The Google analysts found that the interviewing process did not reliably predict which candidate would perform better than others. The only thing it did measure accurately was whether or not the interviewer liked the candidate! Now that was a big problem because managers at Google spent roughly five to ten hours interviewing every new hire. This means that some managers were involved in the hiring process almost on a full-time basis. A lot of time and money was wasted in inefficient interviewing processes. Yet despite all that time and effort managers at Google were not hiring the best people.

The analysis also revealed that multiple interviews with the same candidate did not lead to a better estimation of future performance. After the fourth interview managers were just as good at estimating performance as after the tenth interview.

Even though hiring at Google did not work as it should, everyone still wanted to interview the new guy that was going to replace Jimmy. This was when Google did something quite un-Google-y: they forced a top-down decision and decided that each candidate would undergo no more than four interviews.

So what does this teach us? The way Google hired was traditional. Managers and employees at Google spent over a hundred thousand hours interviewing new candidates in their first ten years. Only after the data analysts ran the numbers was it discovered that their interviewing system was very time consuming without actually leading to better hires. The numbers showed that the interview process needed to become more efficient and more effective.

Google solved this challenge by removing human bias as much as possible. They did this by automating the interview. In these interviews an application called qDroid directs the interview. The interviewer inputs the candidate's function and asks them questions prompted by the app. These questions are formulated by qDroid. This method ensures that the interview is structured. In addition, the fact that interviewers do not formulate their own questions makes the interviews a lot less biased. The questions formulated by qDroid have been extensively tested and have been proven to accurately predict the candidate's job performance.

Furthermore, the interviewers store the candidate's answers in the app. Then they rate the candidate on several very specific scales.

In the end all this information is converted to a single number – a number that has proven to be highly predictive of a candidate's future performance.[1]

The future of people analytics

People analytics is most important for HR and the CEO. HR data and analytics help HR to make better decisions about the way people are managed. This means that it can potentially impact all HR processes, like recruitment and selection (as we saw at Google), compensation, learning and development, and firing. Yet it goes even further than this.

Bloomberg

Bloomberg, a major financial news and data company, sells terminals for 20 000 dollars a year. These terminals provide quick access to the latest news, sales figures and other data. Bloomberg tracks all keystrokes on these terminals, *both for their employees and their customers.[2] The customer information can then be used to provide a better and more streamlined service. The employee information is useful for analyzing how often people work and how productive they are.* Productivity, in this case, is *measured in keystrokes and in this way Bloomberg is able to analyze which journalist produces content the fastest. In addition, Bloomberg tracks when people check in and out of their 192 offices all over the world. Literature shows that people who arrive later at work are more likely to be absent in the near future or even switch jobs! (Griffeth, Hom & Gaertner, 2000)*

Humanize

Another company, Humanize (previously called Sociometrics Solutions), brings analytics even closer to the workers. In order to analyze how people interact and communicate, they are provided with a personal recording device which they can attach to their badges. These devices record people's posture and tone of voice. As such, the company is able to track who talks to who, and in what tone of voice. These badges help companies identify the informal structure in the company; conversations that people have at the coffee machine and during lunch break are very important to how the company functions – but they have never been accurately recorded. Humanize uses all this information to draw social (communication) networks and analyze the quality of the relations between people who interact with each other. According to a Business Insider article on this subject, the company can even track when people are excited about a certain topic.[3] When people talk faster and in a high-pitched voice, they are more enthused than when they talk slower and in a lower tone.

These examples are amongst the more futuristic examples but analytics applies to many day-to-day examples as well. Some questions that can be answered through analytics include:

- What is the return on investment in learning and development? Which groups benefit the most/least?
- Which employees should I hire?
- How should I compensate my employees so they perform at their best?
- What impact do safety policies have on the number of workplace accidents?
- Does our free fitness program actually benefit our employees' health and happiness?
- Which of my employees are most likely to leave the company? And why?

In the next chapters of this book we will give you more examples and enable you to build a process for answering the questions that really matter to you and your organization. Our goal is to make you more familiar with HR analytics, help you understand what it is and show you how it can help your business. In the next chapter we will discuss a brief history of HR analytics.

2.

PEOPLE ANALYTICS: A BRIEF HISTORY

Taylorism: Efficiency is King

In the early 1900s, Frederick Winslow Taylor published a book titled "The Principles of Scientific Management". In his book, Taylor, who was a mechanical engineer, applied the engineering principles familiar to him to the work that was done by factory employees. According to Taylor, workers would be more productive when their task matched their personal capabilities, and when there was a reduction in activities and movements extraneous to the task's completion (Saylor Foundation, 2013)[4].

One of Taylor's followers was car manufacturer Henry Ford. Ford was a successful businessman who had produced many different cars, which he labeled alphabetically (the first being his Ford Model A). Ford's newest car, the Model T, was very popular amongst consumers. In its first year of production Ford sold well over 10 000 vehicles.

This tremendous demand for cars forced Ford to consider more efficient production methods. To achieve this, he hired Taylor to observe his workers and come up with efficiency increasing ways to make new cars. Taylor recommended that larger car parts should remain stationary, while smaller parts would be brought to the car. Ford studied Taylor's observations and applied his principles of scientific management to his production process. Furthermore, he decided that the workers should also remain stationary. The car would physically move from workstation to workstation where workers at each station would perform their specialized tasks before the car was moved to the next station. This process was repeated until the car was complete (EyeWitness to History, 2005)[5].

However, Ford found that, to successfully complete their task, some workstations required more time than others. This led him to recalibrate tooling techniques in other areas to compensate for the longer waiting times (Saylor Foundation, 2013).

Ford continued to optimize this process and in 1913 he had managed to bring the average production time of a Model T down to 93 minutes. As a consequence, Ford was able to lower the Model T's price to 575 dollars and, by 1914, he had captured 48% of the automobile market, selling over ten million cars (Saylor Foundation, 2013). Now, this wasn't all. Since production was so much more efficient, Ford was able to reduce his employees' nine-hour workday to eight hours, while raising their weekly wage from 2.83 dollars to 5.00 dollars (Meyer, 1981)[6].

Human relations movement: why people are important

Taylor's scientific management theory was one of the first management theories that showed the immeasurable business value of optimally deploying human resources. Yet, it also had drawbacks. In the late 1920s increasing unionization enabled workers to publicly protest of their lack of voice and autonomy in the production process, as well as the unforgiving working conditions that forced workers to be at least as fast as their assembly line.

At the same time, American social scientist Elton Mayo was conducting his famous experiments at a plant in Hawthorne. Mayo was studying the impact of lighting conditions on workers, exposing some workers to higher levels of illumination than others. When Mayo measured post-intervention productivity, he found that workers were 25% more productive compared to when he began the experiments. No matter how physical conditions were altered, workers were still more productive. What happened?

By merely asking workers to participate in their experiments, Mayo's team empowered the workers. The workers found themselves to be an important group whose help and advice were sought by the company. This was a revolutionary finding and was coined the Hawthorne effect. Where Taylor focused on production efficiency, Mayo introduced a behavioral element to the productivity equation and gave rise to the human relations movement which proposed that workers would be more productive when their social conditions were satisfied (Wiliamette University, 2016; Chimoga, 2014)[7, 8]. Prominent researchers of the human relations movement were Maslow, whose hierarchy of needs showed how employees can get the most out of themselves, and McGregor with his Theory X and Theory Y. On the one hand, Theory X proposed that people need financial incentives and the threat of job loss in order to work harder, while Theory Y proposed that people are self-motivated and have a need for work and creativity. Both Maslow and McGregor showed that employees' feelings, sentiment and productivity were affected by their work conditions, like the type of leadership style, management or colleagues they dealt with (Chimoga, 2004; Grant, 2010)[9].

Personnel management
The human relations movement instituted an increase in government legislation and worker rights. In addition, both World Wars caused a shortage of workers because many left to serve in the military. This resulted in higher wages and high employee turnover. Companies had no choice but to focus on optimizing worker effi-

ciency, and, in turn, this gave birth to modern personnel management as we know it.

Within the company, personnel management had a caretaker function: It didn't take part in the company's strategy but focused on the management and administration of employees in order to fulfill their work-related needs. Keeping employees content was important, especially because of the unions' rising power during the 1950s in both the United States (U.S.) and Europe.

At the end of the 1960s, the quality of life at work became increasingly important. Organizations started to realize that employee wellbeing played a key part in maximizing organizational performance. During that same time, global student protests showed that the role of power and leadership had changed. Personnel management became more and more involved with job design and enrichment, while greater focus was placed on employee participation (Lievens, 2011)[10]

Human Resource Management
From that point on, history shows a growing emphasis on job enrichment, rapid technological progress, surging global competition, and the rise of the service industry in which employee's skills are very valuable. These factors pressured the personnel department into changing focus from personnel management and administration, to a role that centered on the reinforcement of company policy and culture through people practices. So, as the employee has become part of the company's (human) capital, the core of employee management shifts to growth and engagement, and management practices aim toward getting the most out of people. In addition, HR professionals are now called *business partners* and serve as support to line managers.

Compared to personnel management, an efficient HRM department offers a number of integrated services: recruitment, hiring, firing, learning and development practices, and performance appraisal. These services have become more integrated and in line with the company's vision and strategy, moreover, this integration has been coined Strategic Human Resource Management.

Yet, despite countless attempts from HR managers and directors to transform HR into a more strategic business partner, it remains a support department having relatively low impact on business decisions. On an organizational level, HR is mostly involved with operational and tactical tasks, but fails to have a strategic impact. Attempts to change this and instigate a Chief People Officer, or Chief Human Resource Officer board function have had very little effect until now (Lievens, 2011).

People management and analytics

This is where people analytics enters the stage. Where personnel management focusses on administration and HRM focusses on supporting employees, people analytics brings the science back to HR. People analytics allows HR to quantify its efforts and impact in order to encourage better people decisions. It is, in a literal sense, a revival of *people driven scientific management.*

This idea, that people are best managed by taking a data-driven approach, is new to many HR practitioners. Instead of relying on gut feeling, HR deploys analytics so as to speak the same language as all the other departments in the organization: numbers. People analytics lets HR convert a (people) problem into a numeric rating and a dollar amount. It enables HR to calculate the Return on Investment (ROI) of people policies. An ROI shows the added value of these policies and gives HR the power to show that it can actually help the business earn more money by hiring the right people and making better people decisions. Although reducing a person to a single number sounds scary to some, it offers HR a weapon that aids in establishing its position as a serious business partner. HR analytics and people analytics are strong tools for HRM to become more strategic.

In fact, it's believed that HR can only become a true *business partner* when it quantifies its own impact and actively influences business decisions using data. If not, HR remains a *business assistant* that does important work, without adding to the value and competitiveness of the business.

In the next chapter, we will talk all about HR as a business *partner*.

3.

WHY IS PEOPLE ANALYTICS SO POPULAR?

People analytics or HR analytics?

Interest in people analytics has spiked in the last couple of years. According to Google, around 3 000 individuals search for people analytics every month. This term is most popular in the U.S., U.K. and India. A similar trend is visible for HR analytics, with over 8 000 internet users searching it every month.

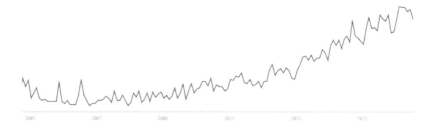

Google Trends (relative interest) on HR analytics. Search popularity has increased over 1600% since 2007. An almost identical trend is visible for people analytics.

People analytics and HR analytics are often used interchangeably. Although the term HR analytics has frequently been employed, there has recently been an increased need to put HR analytics into a broader perspective. At the same time, the term people analytics has become more popular especially due to the rising demand for HR analytics as a separate center of excellence within existing companies. A center of excellence is a team or facility that specializes in a specific topic and shares knowledge, leadership, and best practices on this subject. The teams in these centers of excellence are often multidisciplinary (they include all the different skillsets we mentioned previously, and more) and are not exclusive to HR (and thus prefer to use the term people analytics). This is why the term people analytics has become more widespread.

HR analytics is slightly more specific to HRM, while people analytics is a term more inclusive of other disciplines like we saw in chapter one. In one of his blogs, Lyndon Sundmark defined people analytics as follows "People Analytics is what happens when you apply Data Science and its principles to the realm of People Management".[11] As yet, a scientific definition for people analytics has not been introduced. It is a novel concept and therefore scarcely explored in scientific literature. However, literature on HR analytics is on the rise. According to Heuvel and Bondarouk (2016), HR analytics is "the systematic identification and quantification of the people drivers of business outcomes".[12] In other words: HR analytics is, just like people analytics, a data-driven approach towards employees. The concepts differ on a conceptual level, but in practice they are the same. Since this book looks at people analytics from an HR perspective, we will use people analytics and HR analytics interchangeably.

Workforce analytics is another term that is used. It implies a slightly broader view of the working population, which often also involves financial metrics indicative of workforce efficiency. The last and least commonly used term is talent analytics. It predominantly refers to performance and attrition analytics.

Another term that is used often, is business intelligence. Business intelligence includes the application, (statistical) tools, skills and infrastructure that enables an organization to analyze its information and improve decision making. People or HR analytics is a specific subset of business intelligence: they focus on people data and people-related decision making.

What analytics can bring HR and the organization

The popularity of analytics is intertwined with the growing popularity of 'big data' and 'data mining'. More and more organizations are discovering the value of data-driven decision making, and this trend is also visible in HR. The data-driven approach to HR comes with several advantages which we will discuss in the following sections:

- Evidence-based HR
- Reducing human bias and subjectivity
- A more strategic role
- A competitive advantage
- Employee focus and regulation

Evidence-based HR

As mentioned before, HR has long been regarded as a fee burner. HR policies were often focused on increasing efficiency instead of calculating the impact of these policies on the business. Due to this focus on efficiency, organizations attempted to reduce cost and effort by managing HR as economically as possible.

Still, there is much more to managing people than efficiency alone. The big question is: How effective is HR? People analytics helps HR to define its effectiveness and in doing so provides answers to questions like:

- Will our managers become better managers when they take leadership training?
- Does the sales training we offer have an effect on our people's sales performance?
- Is our current performance appraisal system effective?

- Do our people policies have the effect we want them to have?
- Are we hiring the right people?

In order to answer these questions, we need to run the numbers, just like Google did in our example in chapter one. Google asked the question: Can a hiring manager predict employee performance? According to literature, they could not. Yet, no manager would believe that his hunch about how a new hire will perform was incorrect. Only by running and showing the numbers, could HR prove that the manager's hunch was indeed incorrect and that new hiring practices were necessary. This is evidence-based HR.

During the highly selective training, the U.S. Special Forces predict which candidates are most likely to succeed. Two key predictors are 'grit' and the ability to do more than 80 pushups. Grit proved a more accurate predictor of training success than IQ.

Another example: Wikipedia editors, or Wikipedians, create and edit articles to keep the world's largest encyclopedia up-to-date. Each day, over 800 new pages are created and 3 000 ammendments are made on the English Wikipedia alone. Wikipedia is able to predict who of its 750 000 editors is most likely to stop contributing. I am not sure how Wikipedia acts on this information, but I think a "thank you for your contributions" email could do wonders to show appreciation and re-engage these Wikipedians.[13]

Although it's important to focus more on effectiveness than efficiency, there's more to it than that. HR should focus on making an impact – and analytics is the tool to do this.

Take professional development as an example. On average, organizations spend 1 200 dollars per employee on training and development. This amounts to a yearly spending of 70 billion dollars in the

U.S. alone. That's over two times the amount of money needed to end world hunger.[14]

Do we actually know the impact of these investments? Honestly, most organizations don't have a clue. Even though HR has extensive knowledge about various training programs and suppliers, it cannot give an indication about the training's effectiveness, let alone its impact on people decisions. This has some major implications.

A friend of mine once told me a story about her cleaning business. In order to retain customers, she wanted to raise customer satisfaction. So, she started training the customer service employees to provide higher quality customer care. Contrary to what she had hoped, this had no impact on customer satisfaction (which was measured several times a year).

After talking to several customers she discovered that it was the cleaners who made the biggest impact on customer (dis)satisfaction, not the customer service employees. The cleaners were the ones who worked the customers' homes and offices so they were the ones who had contact with the customers. They needed to be flexible when office workers put in overtime or when home owners came home earlier. This often conflicted with cleaning schedules.

The customer care problem was solved by training the cleaners in customer etiquette and providing them with more autonomy in scheduling. This had a tremendous impact on customer satisfaction and customer retention.

We analyze everything. We've measured the decline of uninsured people since the Affordable Care Act. We measure the click-through rates on our online marketing campaigns. We even measure things as specific as 'food spending at hospitals in Baltimore'.[15] Despite all this we do not measure the impact of HR policies – even though the majority of money within organizations is spent on people. When we start to measure the impact of HR, it will allow the organization to become truly effective. People analytics helps HR to find out which people policies contribute to the business and which do not.

Reducing human bias and subjectivity

We humans are plagued by unconscious biases. For example: an investigation by BBC Radio Five Live tested whether the name on a job application would influence the chances of getting hired.[16]

"White candidates" (John Andrews and Jenny Hughes) were invited for an interview 23% of the time. "Black African applicants" (Abu Olasemi and Yinka Olatunde) were invited only 13% of the time. "Muslim candidates" (Fatima Khan and Nasser Hanif) were only invited 9% of the time.

The success rates of the applicants varied wildly despite their identical applications and CVs. The article suggests that people who make the selection harbor a racist view, however unconscious it may be. And this is in a time when organizations are increasingly and actively trying to promote diversity!

Analytics helps us escape our biases and imperfect decision-making. Daniel Kahneman, one of three psychologist to ever receive a Nobel price, explains this perfectly in his book *Thinking Slow and Fast*. Imagine a single dice with four green and two red sides. The dice is thrown twenty times: which series of colors is most likely to be rolled?

1) RGRRR
2) GRGRRR
3) GRRRRR

As mentioned before, the dice has four green and two red sides. People therefore perceive 'green' to be a more likely outcome compared to 'red'. Since the first option only has one 'green' outcome, and option 2 has two 'green' outcomes, option two seems to be more likely to happen. This is why most people would choose the second option. However, option 1 and 2 are the same, with the exception that option 2 includes one **extra** 'green' roll. This means that option 1 is more likely to happen: option 2 is two-thirds harder to achieve (the chance that you roll a 'green' dice).

This is another example of how (in this case very simple) decisions are exposed to biases that we are not aware of. These biases color our judgement despite our best efforts to make good, rational and fact-based decisions. Like in our previous example, it shows how evidence-based decision-making can help people make better and more accurate decisions. The remarkable thing is that humans are bad decision-makers. The example in chapter one already showed that managers were unable to accurately predict performance. Even if an algorithm is able to predict only 30% of future performance, it already outperforms humans (by far!). This is why analytics gives us the potential to make better decisions and be fairer to everyone.

A more strategic role
Previously, we mentioned that the total human capital cost comes up to nearly 70% of all operating expenses. That is a big number. In addition, we see that the workforce is being revamped. Different skills are needed in an ever rapidly changing world. Indeed, the workforce may not only be the most expensive company asset but also the one to change the fastest.

Furthermore, companies are increasingly aware of the value of top performers. This especially applies to software developers. The productivity difference among programmers is 10X![17] This shows why hiring the right people is so important, and it is one of the reasons why the 'war for talent' will never stop, even during economic downturn.[18] This phenomenon is not unique to the IT branch. In most industries the top 20% of people churn out about 50% of the output. This holds true for writing, inventions, football, police work and other occupations (Augustine, 1979). These exceptional people just do things better than the rest – and we now have the analytical means to identify these people.

These trends also contribute to the growing importance of HR and the role of people analytics. When HR starts to play a more strategic role, it has to be able to show its added value. We saw this in our Google example: by selecting better candidates, analytics enabled the company to build a stronger and more suitable workforce and thus added to the long-term profitability of the company. HR should aid in creating an effective organization and to measure its contributions. On top of that, people analytics enables HR save time and money. By measuring the effectiveness and impact of people policies, HR can save money while contributing more to the business. This will help HR to be taken much more seriously and to develop into a data-driven discipline.

When talking about a strategic role for HR, the last thing I want to mention is the Chief Human Resource Officer (CHRO). The CHRO is a board position which some progressive companies have adopted to provide the HR director a seat at the table in a new role. This means that HR does more than operational and tactical work: the CHRO represents a truly strategic role for HR. The number of CHROs is increasing. A quick search on LinkedIn shows around 2 600 people having a CHRO title in 2016. This is only 1% of the total number of COOs. However, eight years ago nobody had heard of this position, so that's a decent number. Still, the million-dollar question remains: is HR really fit to be strategic? One could argue that the CHRO position is part of the CEO's job. The CEO is responsible for the company's people and culture. This would mean that the CHRO position is a fad and essentially redundant. Over the long term this would mean that HR would remain in its primarily operational role and would use analytics to help the CEO make decisions about the workforce. Only time will tell whether this will happen or not.

Besides having a more internal strategic role, HR analytics helps the organization build a competitive advantage. A competitive advantage is an externally-oriented, organizational benefit often resulting from this more strategic internal role.

People analytics to gain a competitive advantage

Another consideration regarding the value of people analytics is the competitive advantage it offers the organization. As you will discover later in this book, good people analytics should focus on – and help solve – business priorities. In solving these top business priorities, analytics supports the organization's strategy and thus helps deliver on strategic goals. Examples include: having the right people in the right place at the right time, improved product quality, better cooperation and team performance, reduced workplace accidents, higher innovative capabilities, better customer service, increased sales performance, and so on. By aligning analytics with strategic goals, you promote better organizational capabilities to execute the company's strategy in a more optimal way.

Having the capability to do people analytics offers tremendous value. At the same time, people analytical capabilities are tricky to develop because it involves the combination of multiple fields of expertise (which we will take a closer look at in the next chapter). This makes analytics hard to implement for organizations but, once developed, it also enables companies to effectively compete on these capabilities.

Another advantage which is very scarcely mentioned – if at all – can be found when we look at the current state of psychological research. Recent literature emphasizes that people research is very hard to reproduce, a phenomenon that has been coined the *repro-ducibility crisis*.[19] There are several causes to this problem, one of which is the context of the study. It turns out that people's environment and surroundings are very important in how they behave and react. Even small changes in people's surrounding can influence their behavior. This also holds true in companies; making research on engagement, and research on drivers of employee motivation or attrition harder to generalize. Indeed, these reasons will differ from organization to organization. Something like people's reaction to similar (objectively measured) workloads or even work pressure will be perceived very differently at a big 4 service firm compared to a local municipality. We call this 'the importance of context', and we will discuss it further in chapter seven. The additional strategic advantage of people analytics is in the generalizations of these results. Analytics are helpful in making better decisions, not for *any* firm, but for *your* firm.

Employee focus and regulation

A final consideration for the value of people analytics is the employee focus. There is a good case to be made that it is a firm's ethical and sometimes legal duty to take care of its employees. An example of the latter involves Danish companies which are required by law to report how people contribute to value creation, or Dutch companies which have a mandatory duty of care to be a "good employer". People analytics can help firms in this process, as is illustrated in the following text.

Due to the aging workforce, the pensionable age worldwide is steadily rising. Countries like the U.S., Ireland, Spain, Germany and France are increasing the retirement age of workers over the next few decades. This means that people are leaving the workforce at an older age – and have to work longer. In general, these seniors are more frequently absent compared to younger generations.

In an attempt to reduce absenteeism in this age group, a large German multinational heavily invested to reduce the workload for this group by providing additional time off. Seniors had the option to work four days a week and were also given shorter workdays. However, the effectiveness of these costly interventions was disputed.

The people analytics team in this company decided to analyze this specific group using both quantitative and qualitative methods. Research showed that absence for seniors is often caused by chronic illnesses which are more prevalent at an older age.[20] As such, healthy seniors are not necessarily more absent. In line with this research, the team found that the interventions were effective for people who experienced high workloads and work stress (often because of physically challenging work) but they did not make much difference for the majority of this group, most of whom were healthy and liked their job.

Using these findings, the company decided to reverse the measures taken to reduce workload and only focused on the people who experienced their work as physically challenging. These people's jobs were analyzed and the physically intensive elements were eliminated as far as possible. By analyzing and easing their work conditions case-by-case, the company provided a much better solution for the group of seniors who needed it, at the same time saving money overall.

Why isn't people analytics already mainstream?

Only a small minority of companies have fully developed their analytical capabilities. We have already listed a large number of benefits that people analytics provide. Why don't all organizations have a fully developed analytics department?

The answer to this question is complex. There are a number of reasons why HR lags behind the rest of the organization in terms of analytical capabilities. The next few paragraphs will give an overview of the constraints holding back HR. These constraints are also likely to limit the adoption of people analytics within the company you work in.

Lack of skill

The first reason why HR is slow to adopt an analytics approach is a lack of skills. Traditionally, HR has been regarded as a people business. HR professionals have been trained to support the workforce, be a contact point for workers and keep the paperwork in check.

That being said, the skills needed to run an effective HR department have changed over time. Analytical capabilities require knowledge of data extraction, aggregation and data structuring. Since the traditional HR departments lack the IT and data analytics skills to adopt an analytical approach, a lot of organizations struggle to apply people analytics.

Additionally, HR has been unable to capitalize on the statistical background of its workers. A lot of HR workers have a background in psychology or sociology. These social sciences are rooted in quantitative research which involve a fair amount of data analysis skills. However, these analytic skills have been applied primarily for academic purposes, not for the existing people data within companies. On top of that, a lot of HR practitioners are happy to leave these data-driven approaches behind them and finally start 'working with people' when they graduate.

Wall of Boudreau

The lack of skill impacts HR's ability to adopt more advanced analysis. HR is proficient in reporting things like the number of sick days people take, benchmarking performance between departments, and creating scorecards. These descriptive analytics are relatively easy to produce. However, HR is typically unable to engage in more advanced analytics. When HR wants to engage in predictive and prescriptive analysis, it hits a wall.

This 'wall' was first mentioned by Boudreau and Cascio (2010) and has been coined 'the wall of Boudreau'.[21] According to Boudreau, HR gets 'stuck' because it lacks the skills necessary to use more advanced analytical methods.

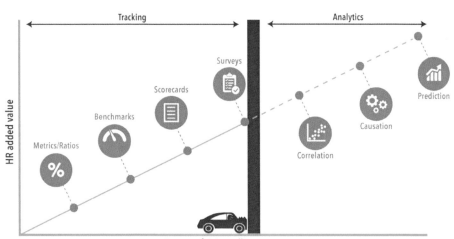

HR often struggles to get past the wall of Boudreau. This is because, on one hand, data from multiple systems need to be combined in order to be properly analyzed while, on the other hand, more advanced data analytics methods are required do the actual analysis.

Examples of predictive and prescriptive analytics are regression analyses, root cause analyses and forecasting. We will talk more about these analytics in chapter nine. In order to do these analyses, HR needs the data processing skills to aggregate and structure data effectively, and it needs a more advanced statistical skillset to actually run the analyses. Only when HR obtains these skillsets will it be able to successfully puncture the wall to develop analytical and predictive capabilities.

The good news is that companies are increasingly combining their existing data sources in new (cloud) data storage solutions. This enables companies to play with people data in existing business intelligence systems and makes extraction of data easier for HR data analytics professionals. This accumulation of aggregated data is one of the drivers behind company-wide analytics efforts and is one of the reasons why interest in people analytics is growing.

The wall of Boudreau shows that HR has to pass through a few 'phases' to develop analytical capabilities. In an effort to help organizations reach analytics maturity, Bersin (by Deloitte) created four talent analytics maturity levels. Organizations that struggle with descriptive analytics have a lower analytics maturity level compared to organizations who are actively making predictive analytics. These maturity levels help organizations to identify where they currently stand, and what they need to do to develop mature analytical capabilities. We will discuss this more in depth in the next chapter.

4.

PEOPLE ANALYTICS MATURITY

Before starting with analytics, it is important to know where you are now. Research by Bersin (2016) found that 92% of companies believe they are not optimally organized for success. It's likely that your organization is part of this majority. Despite (or maybe because of) this, organizations are showing tremendous growth in their people analytics capabilities. This chapter digs deeper into how you can identify where your organization stands and what you need to do to develop full predictive capabilities.

The amount of organizations that use people data to predict performance grew by 125% last year. In 2016, 8% of organizations have used analytics to predict performance thus far (IBM, 2016). Most organizations have not achieved this grade of analytics. Bersin named these different grades 'talent analytics maturity levels'. Most (if not all) maturity models created over time by different companies are based on this model. According to this model, companies can be grouped in four different levels.

At the time of writing this book (late 2016) the majority of companies were at level 1 and 2. These organizations primarily focus on operational reporting. Metrics such as headcount, attrition, cost of labor, absenteeism and attrition are also reported. However, not much is done with this information.

This kind of reporting is part of day-to-day business, and keeping the reporting up to date is usually time-consuming.

There is a high hygiene factor associated with this type of reporting. Hygiene is something that's assumed to be present; when someone has good hygiene it goes unnoticed, but if someone has bad hygiene, people will surely notice. The same goes for HR data: you won't get recognition when the data is up-to-date, but when it's not, you will have a problem. Data-driven decision making is hard for these organizations. Data is often separated in different systems, so combining data to analyze it presents a number of challenges. This is the point where HR hits the wall of Boudreau, which we discussed in the previous chapter.

In level 3 and 4, HR adds increasing value to the business and to strategic decision-making. For example, organizations at the level 4 are able to predict the impact of policy changes based on the data they've collected. This means that HR has all the knowledge and skills to become truly strategic. Furthermore, they have the numbers to back up what they are saying. Organizations at level 4 apply predictive analytics to their workforce. They take their employees very seriously and use them strategically in order to create a competitive advantage.

A slightly different approach taken by some companies involves partnering up with existing analytics providers who then take over part of the company's analytics portfolio. The best-known example is ABN AMRO and iNostix. This means that the organization can start with analytics without having to organize a data warehouse or doing the data analytics themselves. They skip a few levels in the model by hiring external expertise. This approach enables the organization to make data-driven people decisions while internally developing their own data analytical capabilities. It also helps the company to more quickly develop these capabilities, which can be categorized in the different levels we have previously discussed.

Below we attached a self audit that will help you identify the maturity level of your organization. In the rest of the chapter we will discuss the different levels in more detail. Feel free to skip levels which are not relevant to your organization.

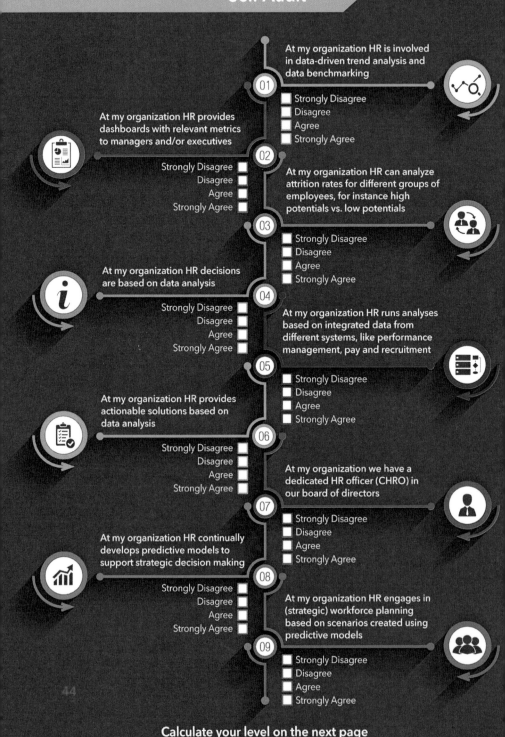

01 At my organization HR is involved in data-driven trend analysis and data benchmarking
- Strongly Disagree
- Disagree
- Agree
- Strongly Agree

02 At my organization HR provides dashboards with relevant metrics to managers and/or executives
- Strongly Disagree
- Disagree
- Agree
- Strongly Agree

03 At my organization HR can analyze attrition rates for different groups of employees, for instance high potentials vs. low potentials
- Strongly Disagree
- Disagree
- Agree
- Strongly Agree

04 At my organization HR decisions are based on data analysis
- Strongly Disagree
- Disagree
- Agree
- Strongly Agree

05 At my organization HR runs analyses based on integrated data from different systems, like performance management, pay and recruitment
- Strongly Disagree
- Disagree
- Agree
- Strongly Agree

06 At my organization HR provides actionable solutions based on data analysis
- Strongly Disagree
- Disagree
- Agree
- Strongly Agree

07 At my organization we have a dedicated HR officer (CHRO) in our board of directors
- Strongly Disagree
- Disagree
- Agree
- Strongly Agree

08 At my organization HR continually develops predictive models to support strategic decision making
- Strongly Disagree
- Disagree
- Agree
- Strongly Agree

09 At my organization HR engages in (strategic) workforce planning based on scenarios created using predictive models
- Strongly Disagree
- Disagree
- Agree
- Strongly Agree

Calculate your level on the next page

Calculate your level

Strongly disagree: 0 points
Disagree: 1 point
Agree: 2 points
Strongly agree: 3 points

Add your points. Your total provides an estimation of your organization's analytics maturity level.

0-5 points: Level 1
6-11 points: Level 2
12-18 points: level 3
19+ points: level 4

Skip to your relevant level to read more.

Level 1

At level 1, HR mostly sticks to operational reporting. 56% of all organizations are at HR analytics maturity level 1.

The HR department seems to be stuck in 'traditional' operational
reporting. This means that they report traditional metrics such as
headcount, attrition, labor cost and training cost. These operational
reports are usually generated with the use of a Human Resources
Information System (HRIS). As was mentioned before, this kind of
reporting is part of day-to-day business and has a high hygiene factor.

How to reach level 2

Level 2 is all about advanced reporting. HR departments at level 2
proactively create relevant reports to support (strategic) decision-

making. They apply benchmarks to HR data to make reports more meaningful. Additionally, metrics are reported multidimensionally, then delivered to management and executives in clear dashboards.

Most organizations at level 1 already use a dedicated HRIS to keep accurate and consistent employee records. If your organization does not use such a system yet, you would do well to adopt it in order to work your way up to level 2. A proper HRIS allows organizations to maintain reliable and consistent data on their employees. This system constitutes a crucial step before beginning with HR Analytics. By using an HRIS, generating reports will become less time-consuming so HR can spend more time on becoming more strategic and working its way to the next level. Moreover, it makes the analysis more reliable. It is not uncommon for level 1 organizations to discuss the data's validity, instead of talking about what the people data shows.

Level 2

HR departments at level 2 are capable of operational and advanced reporting of HR metrics. Around 30% of organizations are at this level while only another 14% of organizations are at a higher level.

At this stage, your organization is able to report proactively. This proactive reporting provides multiple perspectives and is sufficiently advanced to influence (strategic) decision-making. HR reports are descriptive and focused on efficiency. In this case, reporting is part of day-to-day business and still has a high hygiene factor.

In level 2 you should be careful not to invest too much time in generating new HR metrics. Instead, focus on the metrics that offer real strategic value to the organization's main business challenges.

Most organizations at level 2 deliver HR metrics to managers and executives in organized dashboards. It is more important to show relevant information than to show *all* information. Clear dashboards facilitate the translation of HR metrics into useful input for decision-making.

How to reach level 3

Going from level 2 to level 3 primarily deals with the transition from reporting to HR analytics. Analytics is about statistically analyzing HR data in order to develop relevant (predictive) models for better decision-making. In other words, it begs the question: What can we learn from our HR data to make better people decisions in the (near) future?

When applying HR analytics, it is very important to start with a business problem of relevance to the organization. This way time is spent on solving real problems. Hence, remedying these problems will have the greatest impact on the organization.

Applying people analytics will require you to combine different kinds of data. You will need HR data, like demographic, performance and hiring data, but also financial and operational data, from different systems. It is therefore important to have a centralized HR (analytics) department and at least some level of data integration of the various systems. Organizations typically use a business intelligence (BI) system to compound data from multiple systems, or to build up a database of relevant data that can easily be used for analysis.

After putting together all the necessary data, you can start answering questions through statistical analysis. Managers and executives are typically short on time so there is no point in showing them complicated statistical models. To ensure strategic impact, be certain to focus on key business issues and to translate all results into actionable solutions.

Level 3

At level 3, you are part of the top 14%. Only 4% of organizations have a higher HR analytics maturity level. Your organization has surpassed operational and proactive reporting and has succeeded in introducing more advanced analytics! On top of that, your organization uses (statistical) modeling to solve business problems and, based on the data, is even able to predict the future!

As an HR professional working with HR analytics at maturity level 3, you can add tangible value to the organization by proactively identifying issues and recommending actionable solutions.

How to reach level 4

Level 4 is characterized by predictive analytics. Predictive analytics enables organizations to make even better decisions by showing their potential impact. In addition, it will be possible to engage in scenario planning by forecasting what is likely to happen in the future. This allows organizations to mitigate risks more effectively and thus engage in strategic workforce planning: By utilizing predictive analytics, it's possible to tell how the workforce will develop, where leadership succession will be jeopardized and which position the organization will need to fill in the near future.

To make analytics predictive and to move to level 4, you will probably have to add additional analytical capabilities to your team. In a level 4 organization it's likely that you have a dedicated data scientist sifting through your people data. As predictive modeling goes beyond *simple* data analysis, you will begin to use tools that require more programming knowledge. An example of this is R, an open-source system for statistical computation and visualization.

Level 4

At level 4, you are part of the top 4% of organizations.

You are no longer surprised by the feats of HR analytics, because you've seen most of them already. HR plays a major role in your company's strategic decision-making; it is aware of the impact of people policies and actively uses predictive models. In fact, HR is entirely capable of playing a fully strategic role within the company. Level 4 organizations are therefore more likely to have a Chief Human Resources Officer (CHRO) in their Board of Directors, or have a people analytics center of excellence that directly reports to the CEO.

5.

TEAM SKILLSETS

In the first chapter, we mentioned that people analytics is a junction between multiple fields. To apply analytics in the HR field, different capabilities need to be combined in one team in order to show results. These skillsets can be defined under four different contexts:

1) A business context
2) A marketing context
3) An HR context
4) A data analytics context
5) An IT context

People analytics consists of a combination of different skillsets, some of which are rare to find in HR.

We will describe these contexts below and specify the capabilities needed in each context. Only when a people analytics team is able to effectively shift between these contexts will they be a successful and strong analytics team.

It's not necessary to have a large analytics team. Different team members can fulfill multiple roles within the team.

A business context

In order to succeed, the analytics team needs to be connected with the business. This is important because analytics only adds value when it solves a concrete business problem. Only when the team has intimate knowledge of the main business problems, can analytics help to tackle the key strategic issues present in the organization. It is important that the team focuses on real business issues, because it would otherwise run the risk of distracting the business and drowning it in irrelevant numbers. In chapter six we will dive deeper into the identification of the real business issues.

It is a key mistake to begin the analytics process by analyzing data before having a business-driven plan. When the team analyzes data without a clear purpose, they will come up with the most intriguing insights that have no connection with the core business whatsoever. In doing this, people analytics runs the risk of becoming a fancy looking HR showpiece, without inherent value. Analytics is not about the quantity of the data that is gathered, but about gathering the right data to influence decision-making. If there is no analytics plan connecting to one of the company's key strategic challenges, analytics will overshoot its purpose and become irrelevant. The next chapter will explore this in more detail.

In order to become strategic, HR analytics should play a role in one of the organization's top three key strategic issues. Analytics will only help the CEO and CFO when it contributes to the key challenges of the business. So, if the average tenure in the firm is fifteen years, it would not be worthwhile to use people analytics to predict employee flight risk. In this case, employee fight risk is not a pressing issue for the firm, thus would not be a key challenge meriting the CEO or CFO's attention.

However, when done correctly, analytics can have a dramatic impact on the business.

Credit Suisse, an organization with around 48 000 employees, experienced high levels of employee turnover. The costs of turnover proved difficult to calculate but were estimated to run in the tens of millions. By analyzing the factors that predicted employee turnover, Credit Suisse was able to reduce the percentage of people leaving the firm. It turned out that a one point reduction in employee turnover saved Credit Suisse 75 million dollars to 100 million dollars! This is an example of analytics done right, with real impact.

In terms of competencies, the strategic context includes:

- Intimate knowledge of the most important business challenges (outside of HR)
- Solid understanding of key business processes
- Expertise in connecting HR contribution to these strategic company goals

A marketing context

It is not enough just to tackle the key strategic issues. In order to promote meaningful change, HR needs to be able to translate numbers into tangible insights that managers can work with. It needs a marketer's skillset to *sell* analytics. This is more complex than it sounds.

Translating data into actual insights is no simple feat. The way data is presented to people can have more an effect on what people do with it, than the data itself. As such, considering the different ways to present the data before carefully choosing the format will increase the data's impact. You can, for example, present information in a dashboard that managers can log in to, or you can send them an occasional email with a PDF report. Oftentimes, and especially when it is data that does not play an important part of the day-to-day business, managers forget to log into the dashboard and don't look at the data at all. In that case, a monthly or quarterly PDF report sent to their email is more likely to be opened and lead to action than a self-service dashboard. In other words, the effect your data will have depends on the way you present and deliver the data to your target audience.

In addition, your presentation layout also makes a difference in what people do with the information contained therein. Where do you place your graphs? Do you really want to use that speedometer to visualize your engagement score, or is there a better way of presenting that data? Will you use numbers, tables or graphs? What kind of graphs will you use? And, what colors will you use? The culmination of these details exerts an influence on how your analytics results are perceived and whether or not people take action on these results.

It is also important to consider what data you should *not* present. It is tempting to show everyone all your data. Nevertheless, that would result in an information overload for the average manager – they would see the data but won't do anything with it. That being said, effective action is encouraged by presenting only the data which are crucial to eliciting the appropriate action. Nothing more, nothing less.

The way insights are marketed plays an important part in prompting action. This marketing requires a skillset that is of less concern to the average data scientist. To a data savvy person, numbers are self-explanatory facts. However, to most people they are not. The ability to promote your analytical insights in your organization is therefore an essential – and often overlooked – factor in the adaptation of HR analytics.

In terms of competencies, the skillset required for the marketing context includes:

- Understanding how data will be used by the business
- Knowing how and which data add value to the business – and which do not
- Being able to visually present and 'sell' insights

An HR context

Upon commencing HR data analysis, it is important to know what you are doing. A research background in Human Resource Management is therefore vital to the team. Social science focuses on analyzing the factors underlying why people behave the way they do. Genetic attributes, personality and environment influence how people act. Understanding which factors exert influence and how these influential processes work will help you in selecting the right data and in creating a valid, science-based data analysis.

For example, when you want to predict flight risk, there are a number of factors you should consider. Age, tenure, sex, education and seniority are all relevant factors. However, there are many more factors. In the field of occupational psychology, these turnover drivers have been studied intensely since the early 1930s. This knowledge contributes to the identification of the key driving factors of turnover. The literature shows that other factors, like travel distance to work or marital status, influences an employee's intention to leave the firm.

The HR context is also important when it comes to interpreting the analysis' results. Oftentimes these results can seem inexplicable. Being able to interpret and explain these results based on literature will further the accuracy of the analysis.

Previously, I worked with a firm which found out that employee turnover was especially high in their international operating division, but they could not explain why. It turned out that people in these divisions frequently traveled between different countries and spent many nights in hotel rooms, away from their homes. By including the number of hotel bookings per employee into their analysis (frequent international travel is a stress factor), they found that this factor greatly influenced the actual turnover, especially for recently married women in their thirties. Most importantly, this was a factor the firm could influence relatively easily.

In terms of competencies, the skillset required for the HR context includes:

- Having a scientific background in social sciences to discover relevant personnel factors and best practices in research
- Insight in existing HR processes to explain firm-specific findings
- Connecting more traditional HR with people analytics expertise

A data analytics context

Business, marketing and HR focus on the 'softer' side of business. For an effective people analytics team you also need more technical and statistical data analytics skills.

First of all, a data analyst needs statistical knowledge. Simple relational analytics like correlation and regression analyses, but also more complex models like predictive analytics and data mining techniques require a solid understanding of statistics.

When an analyst selects data, he/she has to know what a relevant sample size is, how different variables interact with each other and how these can be included in an analysis. Statistical knowledge is also helpful in selecting the right tools and techniques to do data analytics. For example, when analyzing turnover, you can use a regression model to estimate the most important drivers of employee turnover. On the other hand, you can use a survival model to estimate the chances of employees leaving the company based on certain factors. Both analyses offer interesting results and answer a similar question. Choosing the analysis that best fits the business problem is part of the statistical skillset. We will talk more about different data analysis techniques in chapter nine.

In order to do (statistical) data analysis the analyst needs to be able to work with different software. Tools like Excel and SPSS are well suited for smaller data sets and specific analyses. Pivot tables in Excel lets you quickly sort and retrieve relevant data while SPSS enables you to do relatively simple correlational and regression analyses. However, data analysts often use more complex tools.

Since HR analytics applies best to larger organizations, the size of data sets are also larger. Tools like Excel and SPSS can only handle so much data before they start clogging up your computer's memory, and start struggling with quick data manipulations. This means that data analysis is often done in tools like R, which require a more solid programming background.

R is a tool for statistical computation and graphics. It enables the data analyst to quickly import, manipulate and analyze data through text commands. This makes it less intuitive compared to Excel and SPSS, but it is much more powerful and nimbler in dealing with massive data sets.

In terms of competencies, the skillset required for the data analytics context includes:

- Excellent understanding of statistics
- Understanding various data analysis methods
- Being able to work with software like Excel and SPSS/Stata or other relevant software
- Programming knowledge and experience in working with data analysis and visualization software, like R and/or Python

An IT context

A data analyst's skills are more closely linked to the IT context than any of the other contexts. Depending on the type of analysis, different data are required. So it is beneficial to understand IT structures when aggregating data from different data sources. For example, when a company wants to relate engagement data with performance outcomes, it needs to extract demographic personnel data from the main HR system. Performance data originates from a performance management system while engagement data is most often collected by a third party. Aggregating these different data sources is a challenge that requires a specific set of capabilities. It is not uncommon for analytics teams to request access to real time data for certain dashboards. Moreover, connecting to different APIs requires an understanding of IT structures as well as programming skills.

Given that the data analyst has programming experience, he/she oftentimes has the IT skills needed to aggregate data. That's why the IT context and data analyst's capabilities are often combined.

In terms of competencies, the skillset required for the IT context includes:

- Understanding business IT structures
- Being able to aggregate (real time) data from different systems
- Organization-specific IT skills like SQL server administrator/developer

Why you need all five skillsets

It is tricky to concretely define which skillsets are necessary to create a mature HR analytics team. Previously, we laid out the specific contexts in which these skillsets are used. When the analytics team contains the required business, marketing, HR, IT and data analytics capabilities, they will be able to operate at maximum effectiveness. When one or more capabilities are lacking, they will surely experience difficulty.

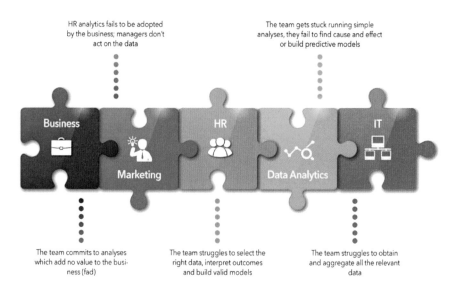

When one or more of the five skillsets are missing, teams tend to run into trouble. By identifying these problems, the team can oftentimes identify in what area they lack capabilities.

A team without a business focus runs the risk of becoming a management fad. It is likely that they will run interesting analyses – analyses which have nothing to do with the business at all. This will turn the HR analytics team into a (rather expensive) fee burner with a short life expectancy.

The marketing focus helps to advocate and 'sell' analytics within the organization. How managers act on data is influenced by the way it is presented. Additionally, different people in different departments and different levels of the organization want to see different things in the data. Having a customer-driven (marketing) approach will greatly aid in promoting analytics. Without this focus, analytics will still provide beautiful insights, but their impact on the business will be diminished due to low adoption.

When a team lacks an HR focus, they run the risk of relying too heavily on the available data. HR analytics is essentially an applied science. As is common in applied science, research (analytics) start with what we already know. Based on this information, hypotheses are created and tested. Without a solid understanding of the social HR sciences it is difficult to test the right models, find the data that matters, and interpret the data in a way that is valuable to the company.

Perhaps most importantly, the team needs data analytic capabilities. These skills are vital to select and clean the relevant data, but also to choose the most appropriate analytics. Without this skillset the team will fail to surpass operational reporting, fail to effectively analyze data, and ultimately fail to apply more advanced strategic and predictive analytics.

Lastly, the team needs IT skills to effectively aggregate data. Without the knowledge of IT infrastructures or the ability to extract data, the analyst will struggle to obtain data from different systems. This will hinder, or even halt the analytics team's progress.

Introduction to the people analytics process

Now, you ask, how does people analytics work?

The people analytics process can be divided in five sequential steps. Every organization has to take these steps in order to successfully apply analytics. Depending on your organization's people analytics maturity level (see chapter three), your HR analytics team might have already taken some of these steps.

The people analytics cycle involves five steps, which are often re-peated multiple times to successfully use analytics to solve a busi-ness problem.

In each of the following chapters we will describe a different step.

- Chapter 6 - Asking the right questions
- Chapter 7 - Selecting the right data
- Chapter 8 - Cleaning the data
- Chapter 9 - The basics of data analysis
- Chapter 10 - Interpretation and execution

Before you start to analyze data, you will need to know what questions you want to answer, or what hypothesis you want to validate. Don't just start with any question: Choose a question that is the CEO's top priority.

Chapter seven will look into how to select your data. The data you select should be compatible and in line with the question you want to answer. When you have selected your data, we will look at how you can clean and order your data. This is the topic of chapter eight. It also includes a checklist that will help you in your data-cleaning process.

In chapter nine we will discuss the basics of data analysis. We will explain the different methods of data analysis and illustrate them with examples. Finally, chapter ten tells of the interpretation and execution of your results.

6.

ASKING THE RIGHT QUESTION

The first step in the people analytics process is about asking the right questions. All research starts with one or more questions or hypotheses. They provide guidance as they structure the entire research project. Your hypothesis influences what data you need to select, how you analyze your data and what actions you take to execute on the insights that the data yields. Thus, this chapter will examine how to ask the right question.

Previously we discussed the importance of knowing the business context. As we mentioned before, it is important to know what the business context is when we start with people analytics. It is critical for the analytics team to be well connected to the business in order to spot and solve the problems the business struggles with. Consider the following example.

The HR director of a large company in the Netherlands was very keen on developing people analytics capabilities. To do so, he created an analytics task force and hired a data scientist. The task force was made up of four highly motivated people who started to dig around in the data. Based on the available data and literature, the team decided to attempt to predict employee churn.

After selecting the relevant variables, the team started to structure and clean the data. After a few months, the team was able to predict which employees were likely to leave the organization within the next year.

This was an amazing discovery and a win for the people analytics team. The team was also able to identify factors that contributed towards employee turnover and could advise manager and HR business partners based on their data. In the end, they created a dashboard that was accessible to key managers inside the organization.

However, this dashboard was very rarely used. Hardly any manager logged into the system and even fewer acted on the information. This puzzled the analytics team. When asked about it, a senior manager said: "I just don't see it as a problem. It is okay when people leave because it gives others in the organization a chance to be promoted to those positions".

The company's average turnover was around 6% (including retirement), which is the Dutch average turnover.[22] This means that the average employee stays with the company for an average of almost seventeen years. The Netherlands has a very loyal workforce. Indeed, the Netherlands has the lowest employee turnover in Europe. The data produced by HR was interesting, but not at all relevant to the company.

Managers did not perceive employee turnover as problematic. Conversely, these managers were often trying to promote and reward their high potentials. When a position would open up this was always welcomed because it would enable them to internally promote their high potentials. The people analytics solution was not in line with the business' primary concern and therefore did not add any value.

Always start with a business priority

People analytics provides both HR and the CEO with tools to produce amazing insights. Once a good analytics team is in place, its success within the organization depends on whether or not it is able to solve important business problems.

If it is unable to do so, it can potentially produce very interesting results which do not benefit the business at all, like you saw in the example above. In order to have a strategic role, the team needs to focus on a real business problem. The team should therefore define the top business priorities within the organization. When these priorities can be solved using people analytics, the team adds real value to the organization.

This point is emphasized in a recent publication on Human Resources analytics by Rasmussen and Ulrich (2015)[23]. According to them, HR analytics begins too often by studying the data without looking at the real challenges that the business faces. This approach greatly diminishes the value of HR analytics. Indeed, Rasmussen and Ulrich warn that this approach could subdue the impact of HR analytics and reduce it to a short-lived craze.

The CEO is not concerned with employee birthdays, nor is he interested in the number of signups for employee benefits programs, optimizing HR's performance, call center volumes or HR delivery costs. The CEO is concerned about whether he has the right people. He is concerned about whether his company will reach its diversity goals and thus avoids bad PR, he is concerned about the cost of turnover, and about reducing these costs when they start to negatively influence the company's bottom line performance.

Of course these topics differ per country and organization. Public organizations struggle more with the costs of absenteeism, while private organizations struggle more with high levels of turnover. As we mentioned earlier, most organizations in the Netherlands do not struggle with turnover. However, employees with long-term work-related disabilities, like burnout, are top of mind. Recent Dutch regulation dictates that a company has to pay disabled employees for twelve years. Paying someone's salary for twelve years equals roughly 500 000 euro. If analytics is only able to prevent a single employee from having a burnout every year, it will already benefit the organization. This is a topic that is top of mind for the CEO.

However, outside of the Netherlands turnover is a much more important factor. In fact, turnover analytics is a starting point for people analytics in many companies in both Europe and the U.S.

I spoke with Jake, managing partner in an accounting firm, in early 2015. His most important problem was attracting the right employees. His second most important problem was retaining these people. It turned out that every year over 20% of the employees left his organization. I asked Jake (somewhat surprised) how expensive he thought it is to replace an accountant. After he deliberated on my question, he estimated it to be around 100 000 euro per accountant.

It turned out that Jake was losing money just as fast as he was losing employees. His organization's turnover was greatly reducing his profit margins, and he wasn't even fully aware of it. There are a number of costs associated with high turnover.

1) Knowledge and contacts are lost: Besides loosing specific (tacit) knowledge, the company loses connections as well. This can be especially painful for an accounting firm like Jake's. When clients stay with the firm for multiple years, chances are that they will have a different accountant multiple times over this period of several years. The new accountant has to become familiar with the client company again, and thus expends valuable time for the customer. Contacts are even more vital for sales people as they can take their clients with them.

In addition, turnover has a large impact on long-term tenders and projects. When key personnel leaves, they take years of (sometimes irreplaceable) knowledge with them.

2) *Negative impact on colleagues: When someone leaves, his/her remaining colleagues will be faced with a (temporarily) increased workload. This can lead to a rise in errors and stress which, in turn, drives absenteeism. Additionally, when a trusted colleague leaves the organization, others are much more likely to re-evaluate their position in the firm and will thus be more likely to leave.*

3) *Onboarding of new hires: Onboarding takes time and money as new employees have to learn the ropes. On average, it takes a staggering 32 weeks before an accountant hits his/her optimum performance level.[24] When the new hire is a recent graduate, this period can even take more than a year.*

4) *Hiring is expensive: Hiring involves a lot of costs. The combined costs (recruitment, assessments, onboarding time and training) can add up to an average of one to four times the employee's annual salary.[25] However, when you hire the wrong person, you are in even deeper trouble. A bad hire can cost you up to five times of his/her annual salary.[26]*

We calculated that 15% of Jake's annual revenue went to replacing and onboarding new personnel. We are talking about more than ten million euro on a total revenue of 80 million euro! If Jake could retain each employee for an additional year, his company would save over two million euro annually.

LinkedIn also looked into the costs of replacing employees. According to LinkedIn's findings, a 1% turnover reduction would save a U.S. company with 10 000 employees roughly 7.5 million dollars a year.[27] This means that for every month an employee stays, that organization would save 750 dollars per employee. These are juicy numbers that provide HR with an excellent business case to implement analytics.

The primary business challenges that organizations face differ between countries but also between industries. A chemical company like Shell puts tremendous emphasis on safety. This emphasis is part of the company culture: when people use the stairs they have to hold the banister, whether they work on an oil platform or in the company's headquarter in The Hague. Using analytics to reduce the number of workplace accidents will benefit an organization like Shell much more than, for example, the average legal firm. This industry faces totally different priorities.

This also emphasizes that, in order to apply people analytics, you should look at the best ways of adding value to the company. This means that the issues you'll work on need to connect with a top business priority and that HR (analytics) should add value to that specific priority.

Why HR should be about creating value
When we take a step back and examine the role of people management within a company, we often see HR struggling to add value to the business. On the one hand HR struggles to create value, and on the other hand HR struggles to show *how* it adds value. In order to become both more beneficial and more strategic to the business, HR should be more concerned about adding value.

Nevertheless, HR practitioners often struggle with defining exactly which challenges they face. When asked what the greatest challenge is that he/she deals with in his/her job, the HR professional usually says something like: "I want to support the line manager", "I want to be taken more seriously by management" and "I want to ensure an uninterrupted flow of personnel".

These are great goals. They are, however, not enough to create value for the business. The question remains as to what the impact is of supporting the line manager, or how to be taken more seriously by management, and why that adds value to the business. In order to create impact, HR should examine its added value. When HR is aware of its added value other initiatives, like people analytics, will also greatly increase in value.

Ulrich and Dulebohn (2015) write that HR practitioners should focus more on the results of their work, instead of focusing on the work itself.[28] In order to achieve this, HR practitioners need to explain why they do what they do. This is best done in a "so that" statement.

"I want to achieve an uninterrupted flow of personnel, *so that* work activities are continued" is a much more powerful statement, because it has a clearly defined purpose. Continuous work activities are important, especially in manufacturing industries. The costs of stopped production, or downtime, in the automobile industry averages around 22 000 dollars and could be as high as 50 000 dollars *per minute*.[29] For these industries, smooth and uninterrupted operations are vital. By inserting a "so that" statement, HR makes its contribution much more tangible.

However, Ulrich challenges practitioners to answer a second "so that" question. "I want to achieve an uninterrupted flow of personnel, *so that* work activities are continued, *so that* department productivity stays constant and downtime costs remains minimal". The second "so that" question forces HR practitioners to really think about their strategic impact and the external content of their work. By having the right hires at the right place and making sure ill employees are replaced before their shift starts, HR reduces downtime cost. Human caused downtime (costs) can even be a measure of the HR's effectiveness. This makes an impact.

According to Ulrich: "We no longer create value by just serving employees, but by making sure that services we offer inside the company align to expectations outside the company". Asking the second "so that" question forces practitioners to take an "outside/in" approach and really pinpoint the value they add to company processes. Doing this is very important.

"As HR professionals understand both the business context and relationships with key stakeholders, they change their conversations with business leaders. The conversation does not start with what HR is about; it starts with what the business is trying to accomplish. An HR professional who was clamoring to be invited to the strategic table and conversation finally got his wish, and he attended the strategic meetings. In the first meeting, the focus was on doing business in emerging markets, and he was not sure what HR could contribute. In the second meeting, the focus was on the economic condition of the organization and managing costs, and again he was silent waiting for an appropriate HR topic. In the third meeting, the focus was on product innovation for the changing societal conditions, and he still waited to comment. He was not invited to the fourth meeting. Knowing the business context and the key stakeholders would have enabled him to engage in strategy conversations without waiting for a more explicit HR topic to come up."

Ulrich, 2015, p. 6.

In order to effectively implement people analytics, the analytics team needs to know what important business issues they are solving. Only when the team is effective in fixing the issues that are foremost in the CEO's mind, does the team add value. The question that remains is how HR adds value to these key business issues.

The tricky thing is that HR professionals find it very difficult to define their added value. In order to identify this, HR professionals should answer why they do what they do, *twice*. This added value is often tremendous, but also invisible. By asking the "so what" question two times HR will have a much easier task in specifying how it adds value to business processes.

Only by answering the "so what" question can HR specify how it adds value to key business challenges like doing business in emerging markets and stimulating product innovation.

7.

SELECTING THE RIGHT DATA

Once you know what questions you want to have answered, you can determine the data you need to conduct your analysis. HR analytics and people analytics are deeply rooted in quantitative science. This means that there are a few key principles that you need to keep in mind when conducting an analysis. These principles prevent you from drawing incorrect conclusions.

There are three key principles you need to keep in mind when you select your data. The first one has to do with the level of analysis, the second with the importance of context and the third with the complexity of the outcomes.

Level of analysis

In organizational research, you have three levels of analysis: the individual level, the group level and the organizational level.

Every variable can be grouped into one of these levels. For example, individual performance ratings say something about the individual. Team performance says something about a group. Revenue says something about the entire organization. These three variables are attributed to different levels.

With every analysis you do it is very important to keep in mind the relevant level of analysis. For example, the individual performance of all team members does not equal the performance of the team. There are other factors at play which influence team performance. When the personalities in the team are not compatible, or people have overlapping skillsets, a team will be less likely to perform well – even though each team member is a star performer. In other words: the individual performance of all team members is an indication of team performance, but certainly doesn't equal it.

In line with this, when all the divisions in an organization perform well it does not mean that the overall organization performs equally well. If the divisions do not cooperate and lack synergy, the organization as a whole is less likely to benefit from the excellent performance of these individual divisions. When you look at divisions separately, you miss the synergies that can take place which can potentially make the whole greater than the sum of its parts.

In other words: you cannot fully deduce the effects of one level, based on variables that say something about another level. For instance, you are less likely to find an effect when you want to relate individual engagement levels to organizational performance than when you want to relate individual engagement levels to individual performance. The level of analysis is therefore very important to keep in mind for every analysis you'll want to do.

To find the strongest effects, you can best stay on the same level of analysis. Of course you can analyze relations that cross a single level, e.g. relate individual engagement levels to team performance, but you should be aware that information gets lost (for example, the synergies that happen when people work together). Analyzing relations from the individual level to the organizational level is much harder to do because you will simply miss too much information. Relating individual engagement levels to organizational bottom line performance is therefore harder to do because, similarly, you will simply miss too much information in your analysis. This will lessen the effect and lead to potentially useless, insignificant results.

The importance of context

When you use people analytics, context is very important. When you want to explain a team's behavior, you need to pay attention to all the factors that play a role in predicting this behavior. However, context goes further than just the level of analysis you use.

Boris Groysberg, a professor of business administration at Harvard Business School analyzed star stock analysts. From 1988 through 1996 he and his team followed 1 052 of the best performing stock analysts in 78 U.S. investment banks. These stars helped their company earn millions and millions of dollars. No wonder that these companies were very competitive in hiring these stars from other firms.

In contrast, Groysberg found that when a star was hired by another company, his/her performance plunged. Goysberg's data showed that 47% of analysts did poorly in the year after they left their firm. Performance dropped by about 20% and did not recover, not even after five years!

> *"There's no dearth of examples: James Cunningham, who was ranked Wall Street's top specialty chemicals analyst from 1983–1986, dropped to third place as soon as he left F. Eberstadt for First Boston. Likewise, Paul Mlotok, who specialized in tracking international oil stocks, dropped from number one in 1988 to number three the following year, when he moved from Salomon Brothers to Morgan Stanley."*

Harvard Business Review, May 2004[30]

Now, why did the performance of these star analysts drop as soon as they switched jobs? What happened is that these stars' performance is only partially explained by their personal skills and capabilities. James Cunningham was still a very smart and capable analyst after joining First Boston. However, he was not the best anymore.

In order to explain this, you need to consider the context. An analyst is not a one-man band. According to Groysberg and colleagues (2004), the systems and processes of their firms and the teams that support them, greatly add to their success. When they leave their company, they cannot take these organization-specific resources with them. Learning how the new system works can take years.

> *"Resentful of the rainmaker (and his pay), other managers avoid the newcomer, cut off information to him, and refuse to cooperate. That hurts the star's ego as well as his ability to perform. Meanwhile, he has to unlearn old practices as he learns new ones. But stars are unusually slow to adopt fresh approaches to work, primarily because of their past successes, and they are unwilling to fit easily into organizations. They become more amenable to change only when they realize that their performance is slipping. By that time, they have developed reputations that are hard to change."*

Harvard Business Review, May 2004

When you see something happen within your organization you should always ask yourself about the context in which it happened. This holds especially true for performance ratings. In general, we tend to underestimate the influence of external factors, and overemphasize the role of internal factors. This means that we attribute both good and bad performance mostly (or exclusively) to the person's judgement and skills, while we forget the importance of the environment and the role of colleagues and bosses. This is such a fundamental error of judgement that psychologists call it the fundamental attribution error.

Stock traders have a saying about this, which is attributed to Humphrey Neill:

Don't confuse brains with a bull market.

In other words: when stock prices are rising, even the biggest idiot can make money. I think this is an important lesson for anyone who engages in analytics: Always keep the context in mind.

Complexity in outcomes

Selecting the right data sources is key to conducting your analysis. How would you define performance? Is it the number of sales? Is it customer satisfaction? Is it manager-rated performance?

These are real questions. Sales employees can receive a favorable rating from their manager, but if their sales numbers don't add up, they are not useful to the organization. Or are they? With the previous examples in mind, how do these sales people contribute to the team and support others in their sales efforts?

These are questions that you have to start asking, before you start your analysis.

It is important to keep in mind that if performance goals are complex, you should pay special attention to the outcome. Let me explain this by using an example.

If you want to know which team is best at playing ice hockey, you should not look at who wins most of the time, neither should you look at who scores the most goals. You should look at who has the most 'shot-at-goal' (SAG) events. Let me tell you why.

On average, a National Hockey League team scores 450 goals, has 5 000 shot-on-goals (SOG) and 9 000 SAG. Whereas SAG includes all shots directed toward the goal, SOG counts only the shots that got stopped by the goaltender or that scored a point. This means that for every game won, 2.3 goals are scored, 7.8 SOG en 10.6 SAG occur.

Since there is so much more data when you look at SAG compared to who wins (10.6 times as much, to be precise), the role of luck (or randomness) is significantly reduced. When a team gets a lucky shot and scores the winning goal it doesn't necessarily mean the winning team is better. Shots-at-goal are a much more frequent and therefore a much more reliable measure of team success, simply because the role of luck (which acts as noise in the data) is reduced.[31]

This example will make you look differently at how you measure sales, especially when you talk about complex 'solution sales'. The sales cycle in business to business solution sales can take up to 1.5 years. Like in hockey, there are other metrics that predict sales success better. Examples could be the number of contacts a sales person has or the number of phone calls he/she makes.

Thus, complexity in outcomes means that the more complex (and rarer) it is for your work to have a successful outcome, the closer you should pay attention to how you can reliably measure success.

Another example: Say you want to predict long-term absenteeism for a company. The company sends you a dataset of 5 000 employees, including the number of absence days per month. Average absence is around 7% and less than 1% for long-term absence. That is less than 50 people in a total population of 5 000. Short or mid-term absence may be a much more accurate measure, because frequent short and mid-term absences greatly increase the chance of long-term absence. The variables are therefore related. Furthermore, short and mid-term absence are much more prevalent in the dataset. Luck (or rather, bad luck) plays a much smaller role in the short-term absence data, and since this data is more abundant it is beneficial in explaining and predicting absenteeism.

8.

DATA CLEANING

After you've thought about which analyses you want to run and identified the specific data you need for these analyses, you'll get to the next step: data cleaning. This is a very important step. A common saying in data analysis is: "garbage in, garbage out". You can put a lot of thought and effort into your data analysis and come up with lots of results – but your results will mean nothing if the input data is not accurate. In fact, the results may even be harmful for your workforce because they misrepresent reality. This is why clean data is so important.

Why data cleaning is important

HR data is oftentimes dirty. Dirty data is a data record that contains errors. This can be caused by different things. Data can be missing, the same functions may have multiple and/or different labels, there may be multiple records for the same people in multiple systems which do not perfectly match, and so on.

Cleaning and ordering this data can be a time-consuming process. Indeed, aggregating data from all these different data sources and making them compliant can take weeks or even months. This holds especially true for multinational companies which often use different systems in different countries to record the same data. As soon as data collection procedures differ in the slightest, the data will become inconsistent.

Of course you can start cleaning *all* your data at once. However, this can take tremendous amounts of time so it is much smarter to carefully select and clean only the data you need to perform a specific analysis. This approach will prevent a lot of unnecessary work and produce results faster. Based on the outcomes of the first analyses, you can determine which data you need to clean in order to run your next analysis.

Data management

When you are working with and cleaning the data, you will inevitably change it; e.g. you manually add a missing record or change a misspelled name. Depending on the quality of your HR data this data cleaning phase can take of lot of time but will also improve your data quality. Higher data quality will lead to more accurate analyses. This also means that you end up with a dataset with data that is more valuable than the data originally extracted from the system. Since this data is of a higher quality, it's preferable to store it in a manner conducive to later use.

In addition to this, the way organizational data is managed influences how you will collect your data and conduct your data analysis. It's more likely that companies with more mature HR data warehousing systems (like a Human Resource Integration System) have already combined data from different data sources, while companies without a data warehouse have to combine datasets first, before they can run an analysis.

If such a data warehousing system is not available, the data has to be extracted directly from the different systems. For example: when you want to analyze which hires perform best, you will have to combine the data from the applicant tracking system with your performance management system. This way you can examine how personality, education, working background, and other factors can potentially influence someone's performance – thus helping you to specify the attributes you need to focus on in the selection procedure.

In this example, data is extracted from two different systems. As discussed before, it is not uncommon for data to have multiple mislabeled functions or section names. These inconsistencies have to be fixed before the data can be combined and effectively analyzed. Additionally, the two datasets need to be merged. This can also take quite some time. A full explanation of data management goes beyond the scope of this book, but remember: when the data is cleaned, this data should either be separately stored or should be fed back into the system. This will help improve the data quality and is extremely beneficial for later data analyses and data aggregation efforts.

The data cleaning process

The data cleaning process can be split up in two major parts, which are referred to as the validity and the reliability of data. When data is not valid or reliable, it may tell you something other than what you were looking for. The following section describes this.

Validity

Validity assesses whether you're actually measuring what you need to measure. Does the appraisal system only measure individual performance, or does it measure who is best liked by his/her manager? Is data collected evenly throughout the organization, or is it skewed in one way or another?

The city of Boston made an app that their drivers could install on their smartphone. The app would measure bumps in the road and report their location via GPS. These bumps were then recorded and the city road service would fix them. According to a spokesperson: "[the] data provides the city with real-time infor-mation it uses to fix problems and plan long-term investments".[32]

However, not everyone benefitted equally from this system. The app was used by the young and in more affluent communities, while the poorer communities did not have equal access to smartphones and mobile data. This is a significant bias in the data.

Questions you can ask yourself in this context, are:

1. Does the data represent what we want to measure?
2. Are there any significant biases in the way we measured our data?
3. Was the data collected in a clear and consistent way?
4. Are there outliers in the data?

Reliability

Reliability is about measuring the same thing over and over again and achieving the same result. When you measure someone's engagement in the morning you want to have a similar result as when you measure it again in the afternoon. This is because engagement is a trait that is relatively stable over time. The same holds true for different raters. If you ask both Bill and Jim to rate Wendy's engagement, you want both Bill and Jim to give Wendy the same rating. However, when the scales that are used to rate Wendy are vague and open to different interpretations, Bill and Jim will likely give Wendy different ratings. This is called a rater bias, which is best avoided.

This might sound obvious but it is not. Oftentimes reported data depends on other factors like the instructions that are given, and the mood of the person who gives the rating. This is the big question when we talk about reliability: Are the same scores achieved when the same data is measured in the same way by different people and at different times of the day/week?

Procedures play an important role in this process. In rating performance, if one manager considers a worker's performance over the last six months, while another only thinks back over the last two weeks, the ratings will likely differ significantly and be unreliable. Clearly documented procedures would help different managers measure performance the same way.

Questions you should ask yourself in this context, are:

1. Did we consistently produce the same results when the same thing was measured multiple times?
2. Did we use clearly documented data collection methods and were the instructions followed each time?

A simple data cleaning checklist
The previous questions on validity and reliability help you to analyze whether your input data is sufficiently accurate to yield productive results. There are several other criteria your data needs to comply with. For example, your data needs to be up to date.

Data that is outdated will produce irrelevant results and can potentially mess up all your work. Additionally, you need to check if you have all the relevant data: records are oftentimes missing. Depending on how you analyze your data, this may or may not cause problems. Some methods of analysis allow for missing data while other algorithms struggle when data is missing.

Missing data will narrow your population. Plus, there is a real chance that there are shared similarities between the people whose data is missing. For instance, if one department still uses an outdated performance management system which omits certain questions, it would mean that you'd lack data of all the people working in that department. This can seriously skew your results towards the other departments and threaten the generalizability of the results.

This is a very practical checklist with six common steps for data cleaning:

1) Check if the data is up-to-date.
2) Check for reoccurring unique identifiers.
    a. Some people hold multiple positions and it's possible that separate records were created for each position, thus they end up having multiple records in one database. Depending on the situation, these records may be condensed.
3) Check data labels across multiple fields and merged datasets and see if all the data matches.
4) Count missing values.
    a. When missing values are over represented in some departments or in specific parts of the organization, they may skew your results.
    b. In addition, an analysis with too many missing values (i.e. insufficient data) runs the risk of becoming inaccurate. This also impacts the generalizability of your results.
5) Check for numerical outliers.
    a. Calculate the descriptive statistics and the values of the quantiles. These enable you to calculate potential outliers. There are multiple methods to do this. The simplest involves multiplying the difference between quantile 3 (Q3) and Q1 by 1.5. The result can be added to Q3 and subtracted from Q1. Values outside this range are assumed to be outliers.

6) Define valid data output and remove all invalid data values.
    a. This is useful for all data. Character data is easily defined (e.g. gender is defined by M or F). These are the valid data values. Any other values are presumed to be invalid. This data can be easily flagged for inspection by using a formula.
    b. Numeric data is often limited in range (e.g. working age is between 15 and 100). Numeric data that falls outside the predefined range can be flagged the same way.

Data Cleaning Checklist

Up-to-date data
Data should be up-to-date in order to obtain maximum value from the data analysis.

Duplicates
Duplicate IDs indicate multiple records for one person, e.g. someone holds multiple functions at the same time.

Check IDs
Check data labels of all the fields to see whether some categorical values are mislabeled.

Missing values
Count missing values and analyze where in the data they are missing. Missing values can disrupt some analyses and skew the results.

10101010
00100010
0011

Numerical outliers
Numerical outliers are fairly easy to detect and remove. Define minimum and maximum to spot outliers easily.

Define valid output
Define valid data labels for categorical data. Define data ranges for numerical variables. Non-matching data is presumably wrong.

9.

THE BASICS OF DATA ANALYSIS

In this chapter we will dive into the actual analytics. First we'll discuss the three main categories of data analysis followed by several examples of different data analytic techniques. Data analytics is all about finding relationships between variables. For example, a lot of people talk about how important employee engagement is for performance. Data analytics can be used to see how engagement (variable 1) impacts performance (variable 2). There are multiple ways of analyzing how one variable relates to another and a few of these ways will be exemplified later.

The three main categories of data analysis are descriptive, predictive and prescriptive analytics. These analytics form the basis of people analytics and business intelligence in general. As we mentioned at the beginning of the book, business intelligence refers to the techniques and tools used to derive useful insight and information from raw data. People analytics is a specific example of business intelligence.

Descriptive analytics
Descriptive analytics is the simplest class of analytics; the analysis gives insight into the data. E.g., descriptive statistics can show you how many employees left the company last month, and how much this number increased compared to the month before. These ana-

lytics are well known for most people as they can be done using standard reporting tools.

This type of analytics enables the user to summarize what happens and see how different data is correlated, such as: traditional dashboards, scorecards and business reports. Descriptive analytics is often referred to as 'slice and dice', as it enables the user to play with the data by calculating the population size, mean, median, minimum and maximum, frequency, etc. of their data(set). Some business tools that provide descriptive analytics are Excel (pivot tables), Qlik Sense and Tableau.

Predictive analytics

As a more advanced class of analytics, predictive analytics can, for instance, show you how many people are expected to leave in the *next* month and how many more are expected to leave the months after.

Predictive analytics answers the questions "what will happen?" and "why will it happen?". These analytics provide a much more tangible grasp of the data by enabling the user to predict, or forecast, what is likely to happen. As you can imagine, these tools can be very powerful and, when applied correctly, have the potential to directly impact decision-making. For example, when you want to predict which employees are likely to leave your company, or how investments in learning and development will impact next year's performance, you are applying predictive analytics. This sort of analytics can be regression analysis or more advanced machine learning techniques, like decision trees, neural networks and Naïve Bayes. Performing these analytics require advanced to expert knowledge in statistics and data analysis, as well as the use of tools like SPSS, R and Weka.

The term "machine learning" refers to a technique wherein computers have the ability to learn without being explicitly programmed to do so. That is to say, machine learning can be considered as a form of artificial intelligence (AI) as it provides computers with the necessary tools they need in order to absorb and learn from new information. The more advanced predictive analyses often involve machine learning.

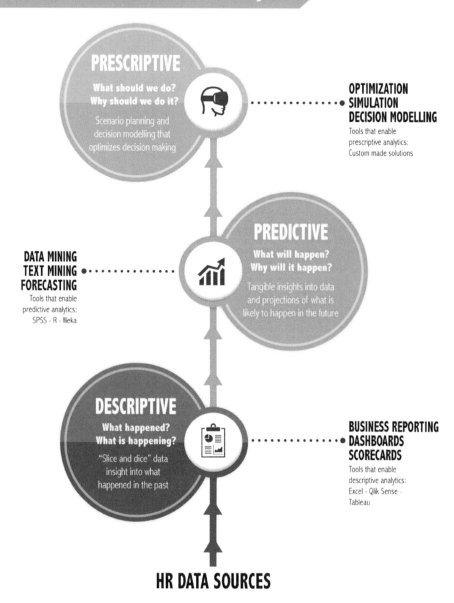

Business Analytics

PRESCRIPTIVE
What should we do?
Why should we do it?

Scenario planning and
decision modelling that
optimizes decision making

OPTIMIZATION
SIMULATION
DECISION MODELLING
Tools that enable
prescriptive analytics:
Custom made solutions

PREDICTIVE
What will happen?
Why will it happen?

Tangible insights into data
and projections of what is
likely to happen in the future

DATA MINING
TEXT MINING
FORECASTING
Tools that enable
predictive analytics:
SPSS - R - Weka

DESCRIPTIVE
What happened?
What is happening?

"Slice and dice" data
insight into what
happened in the past

BUSINESS REPORTING
DASHBOARDS
SCORECARDS
Tools that enable
descriptive analytics:
Excel - Qlik Sense -
Tableau

HR DATA SOURCES

94

Prescriptive analytics

The most advanced class of analytics is prescriptive analytics. Prescriptive analytics gives advice and helps you take appropriate action. Where predictive analytics tells us: "There is an 80% chance that one of your data scientists will leave in the next three months", prescriptive analytics tells us: "Put the job description online this week, so you have a new data scientist in three months' time".

Prescriptive analytics has been coined the "future of analytics" by Gartner, and defined as "the combination of optimization, rules and data that enhances analytics by suggesting the optimal way to handle a future situation and can be applied to strategic, tactical and operational decisions."[33] Prescriptive analytics should help to make sense of data and insights by answering the question "What should I do?". Prescriptive analytics helps you choose the people policies with the greatest impact on the workforce, depending on the specific situation you're in. However, these analytics are still relatively novel in the analytics space.

In the next section, we will give you some examples of descriptive and predictive analyses in order to give you a sense of how they work. Although we tried to keep it as simple as possible, this section will be quite statistical. Don't worry if you don't fully understand everything as we only try to give you a sense of how some of the commonly mentioned analyses work.

Example 1: Correlation analysis

Correlation is a technique that shows how two variables relate to each other. Correlation is a relatively simple example of descriptive statistics.

When two variables are correlated, they have a 'shared variance'. In simple English, the data in the variables are associated with each other.[34] When the value of one of the two variables changes, the value of the other one is also expected to be different. However, as we briefly discussed in the previous paragraph, correlation is *descriptive*, it does not predict anything, but describes how variables are linked.

A small company with ten employees measures performance every year. You can find an overview of the employees, their gender and rank below. As you can see, there are three ranks in this firm (junior, middle/medior and senior) and performance is expressed as a number ranging from 0 to 100.

Employee	Gender	Rank	Perf. Rating
1	M	Senior	90
2	F	Middle	90
3	M	Middle	85
4	F	Junior	60
5	F	Junior	40
6	F	Junior	80
7	F	Middle	65
8	M	Senior	88
9	M	Senior	95
10	F	Junior	75

One of the first things you will notice is that males seem to score higher on performance ratings compared to females. In order to prove that this holds true, we can run a correlation analysis to find out whether your eyes are playing tricks on you, or if both variables are really statistically associated with each other.

The correlation analysis shows that gender and performance are indeed significantly correlated with each other. In this example, the correlation (expressed in Pearson's *r*) is 0.64, which is considered a moderate correlation. In other words: there is a correlation between someone's gender and their performance rating in this example.

A correlation of 0.64 indicates that around 41% of the variance in one variable (gender) can also be found in the other variable (performance rating). The 41% is known as the coefficient of determination, r^2 ($r^2 = 0.64^2 = 0.41$). This value tells us how much of the variability in performance is shared by the variance in gender.

Remember, we are still talking about *descriptive* analytics. We cannot say anything about (causal) predictions.

This is one of the most important lessons on correlation. Correlation does not equal causation. You cannot say that someone's performance is lower because they are female. It is more complex. Let's look at that.

If you look at the data again, you see another pattern. You see that all males but one are senior, while the majority of females are junior. Maybe it's not gender that determines who performs better or worse, but the employee's rank.

This would make sense. Performance is often rated by someone who is more senior. The juniors are rated by the mediors, the mediors by the seniors, but the seniors can only rate each other's performance. It is not uncommon for people with higher ranked jobs to also receive better performance ratings – which is counter intuitive because those jobs are also tougher. This also holds true for this example. When we account for a person's rank, the correlation between gender and performance becomes non-significant. This means that there's no difference in performance ratings between man and women, instead the difference lies in performance ratings between more senior and more junior employees.

The take-home message: (1) correlation does not equal causation, and (2) always look at your data a second time because you may have missed something.

Example 2: Regression analysis

The regression analysis is a more complex statistical technique. It can be used to analyze an outcome using one or multiple predictive variables. The regression analysis can be used as both a descriptive and a predictive analysis, depending on how it is used. Let's look at how the regression analysis works using a different company with around 500 employees.

HR manager Jill has long suspected that many employees take sick days when the weather outside is nicer – but she couldn't prove it until she learned about the regression analysis. Over the last ten days Jill wrote down how many people were calling in sick, and the maximum temperature on that specific day. Here's what her data set looks like:

Day	Temperature		# sick
	C	F	
1	10	50	8
2	15	59	7
3	18	64.4	9
4	26	78.8	15
5	31	87.8	18
6	32	89.6	20
7	29	84.2	20
8	15	59	19
9	16	60.8	12
10	18	64.6	11

In order to find a relationship between temperature and the number of people calling in sick, Jill used a regression analysis to predict the number of absentees by using the temperature as a predictor. In doing so she got the following model.

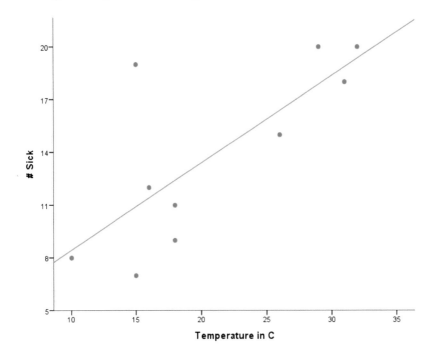

In this picture you see a scatterplot with a line, called the line of best fit. What does best fit mean, you ask? Pretend that all the points on the graph are houses. We need to build a straight road and ensure that the walking distance from each house to the road is as short as possible on average. This way, most of the inhabitants don't have to walk a long way to the road and the most people will be happy. It best fits their need to be close to the road. Similarly, if you were to draw a straight line from left to right in the graph above, this particular line should be the shortest distance to all the points in the graph.

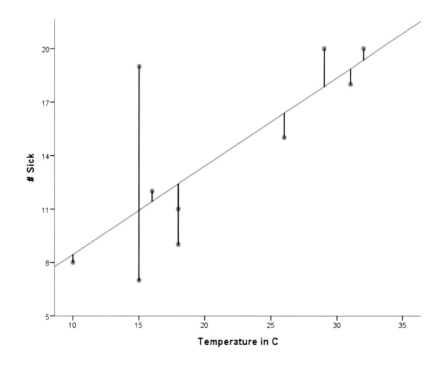

The line with best fits represents the shortest routes (shown in black lines) from all individual data points.[35] This is the regression line.

This line is also called the regression line. It's important because it shows how changes in one variable (e.g. temperature) can affect the other (e.g. sick days). The formula for this line is:

$$Y = constant + a_1 * x$$

a_1 is the value of variable x. It is possible to add multiple explanatory variables to the equation. The formula for this specific line is:

$$\# people\ calling\ in\ sick = 3.48 + .568 * temperature\ (in\ C)$$

Our analysis implies that there is a significant causal relationship between the increase in temperature and the number of sick days. In Jill's (small) data set a temperature change of 10 degrees results in approximately six more people calling in sick. This is a significant effect – but we do not know how this relationship precisely works. There are a number of possible situations. Maybe employees call in sick to go to the beach, or maybe employees don't sleep as well when it's hot and thus fall ill more frequently. To explain precisely how this relationship works we need to do more research. However, our data already enables us to act on it.

When Jill sees that next week is going to be a really hot week, she knows that she can expect an increase in absence – and she can thus call in a few extra employees who can cover for the absentees.

Side note: In order to build a much more accurate and reliable model, we need more data. The problem with the current approach is that the regression line's accuracy is tested on the same data set that was used to create the line. That's very much like a student who marks his/her own paper: in order to get an objective estimation of this student's skills you'd prefer someone else to mark the paper. That's why you want to test your regression line on fresh data to check its algorithm. In addition, we would want to gather a lot more data to build a more accurate algorithm. More data is better in this case.

Example 3: The decision tree

A common and rather simple method of creating a predictive model is the decision tree. A decision tree is a tree-like model consisting of decisions and their possible consequences. In a decision tree, every node represents a test on a specific attribute and each branch represents a possible outcome of this test.

Let's take a different dataset. Imagine your neighbor Paul bought the new BMW Z4 convertible. Since he bought it he's taken every chance he's gotten to drive his new convertible.

Given that you'd really like to have that model car as well, you wanted to see how often Paul drives the BMW. For the first fourteen days, you wrote down how often Paul went out and drove his new convertible. For the sake of this example, you also wrote down the weather forecast, temperature and humidity on a piece of paper.

Your piece of paper looks like this:

Day #	Outlook	Temperature	Humidity	Driving
Day 1	sunny	hot	high	yes
Day 2	sunny	hot	high	yes
Day 3	cloudy	hot	high	no
Day 4	rainy	mild	high	no
Day 5	rainy	cool	normal	no
Day 6	rainy	cool	normal	no
Day 7	cloudy	cool	normal	yes
Day 8	sunny	mild	high	yes
Day 9	sunny	cool	normal	no
Day 10	rainy	mild	normal	no
Day 11	sunny	mild	normal	yes
Day 12	cloudy	mild	high	no
Day 13	cloudy	hot	normal	yes
Day 14	rainy	mild	high	no

Could you predict whether Paul will drive his convertible on any given day? This is where the decision tree comes in. By using a decision tree algorithm you can create a decision tree. With every new branch our decision tree algorithm uses the criteria of information gain vs. default gain ratio per attribute, and then selects the best attribute to split on. Let me explain this.

Decision Tree Example

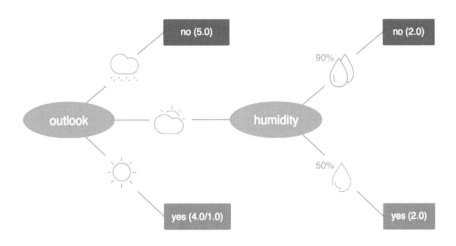

In our example, the weather outlook is the single best predictor of whether or not Paul will take his car for a spin: outlook is the variable with the largest discrimination information (also called information gain). All five days when the outlook was rainy, Paul didn't drive his car. Four out of five times when the outlook was sunny, Paul did drive his car. However, when the outlook was cloudy, the outcome was fifty-fifty. The second best predictor in this example is humidity. Since the information gain ratio of outlook is the highest, that is the variable where the tree first forks. It then forks at the second best predictor, the third, and so on. In this specific example, temperature did not help the algorithm predict the outcome more accurately, so this factor is omitted in the final decision tree.

In other words: the weather forecast and humidity can be used fairly accurately to predict whether Paul will take his convertible out for a spin. The great thing about a decision tree like this is that it clearly visualizes how the decision sequence works. Paul only takes his car for a ride when it is sunny, or when it is cloudy but humidity is low (which is often the case when the weather is nicer).

Even though this simple example might seem very logical, it does show how predictive analytics works. Algorithms that learn from existing data are used to make specific predictions about the (near) future – a process called data mining. Eric Siegel (2013) compares this to a salesperson. Positive and negative interactions teach a salesperson which techniques work and which do not. In a similar way, predictive analytics is a process that enables organizations to learn from previous experiences (data).

Example 4: A random forest

In the previous example we wrote about decision trees. A decision tree enables you to make predictions and visualizes the path an algorithm takes to arrive at this outcome. However, there are even more advanced decision tree algorithms. An example is the random forest. Just as a forest represents a large collection of trees in real life, so does it represent a large number of (slightly different) decision trees when considering machine learning. This is again an example of predictive analytics.

A single decision tree is created by calculating which of the attributes is most predictive for the specific outcome. It's at this attribute where the decision tree will fork. In our previous example, the outlook was the best predictor, so the first fork of the decision tree will occur at that attribute. The next split will occur at the second best predictor, and so forth.

In a forest, these decision trees do not necessarily fork first at the most predictive attribute, but split at attributes in a randomized order. This produces a large amount of different decision trees that all try to predict the chosen outcome.

Now this means that one algorithm has a lot of different trees which predict different outcomes. The random forest algorithm reaches its decision by taking a majority vote between all the different trees. The outcome with the most votes, is most likely to happen – and is often more accurate compared to a single decision tree.

However, it's often quite difficult to see how the algorithm came to its prediction because this is the result of many different decision trees combined. That's why it's (almost) impossible to visualize all these trees and infer how the algorithm came to its prediction.

10.

INTERPRETATION AND EXECUTION

We have arrived at the last step of the HR analytics process cycle: interpretation & execution. In the previous steps we defined a question that is relevant to the business, selected and cleaned the relevant data, and then analyzed it. Using the results of our analysis, we can now continue to the final step: interpretation and execution.

Checking the results

Since people analytics is a complex undertaking, there is a lot that can go wrong during the process. After finishing the analysis there are a few questions you should ask yourself:

- *Is what we are seeing causational or correlational?*
  With every finding you should pause to examine whether it's causal or correlational. Most findings are correlations, and as you saw in the last chapter, you should tread with the utmost caution when you want to deduce causation from a correlational finding. Often there are other variables that play a key role in explaining each correlation you find – and these variables may not have been included in your analysis.
- *Have we adjusted for context?*
  In chapter six we wrote about the importance of context. Context is important when assessing and comparing em-

ployees. Is superior performance caused by the individual employee's world-class capabilities, or does the team around him also contribute to his success? Additionally, are the effects you're seeing isolated, or does the environment in which the company operates exert an influence that you didn't take into account?

These considerations are especially important when you compare people with each other. Are people able to achieve their full potential, or is their manager holding them back? When you compare two employees with different managers, the manager becomes an important part of the context. Environmental factors also play a role. When you do attrition analysis but do not take the national labor market into account, it will be hard to explain why employees are less likely to churn in one year compared to the next.

- *Did our expectations influence the outcome?*
  The self-fulfilling prophecy is a well-known phenomenon in which outcomes are influenced by the expectations people have. Students who are perceived by their teacher to be smarter, are unconsciously given more attention by the teacher and end up performing better – thus confirming the teacher's initial hypothesis. The self-fulfilling prophecy also applies to manager's expectations and might influence your expectation as well. When you expect a certain outcome you are more likely to look for and include evidence that confirms your hypothesis, and ignore and exclude evidence to the contrary.

Part of the first step is re-analyzing your results: Did you really find what you were looking for? Or did you find an answer to a different question? On top of that, did you look at the data in a smart way and take all relevant factors into consideration? If not, you should go through the analytics cycle again and revise your analysis.

Interpreting results

The second step involves the interpretation of your results. This step goes hand in hand with what we discussed in the previous section. Do your results answer the questions that were asked at the beginning of the analysis? Often, one or more new questions pop up, which need to be answered before the results can be accurately interpreted. By going through the people analytics cycle again you can answer these new questions and form a more complete answer to your original question.

Always take a second look at your data when you stumble upon an interesting finding. A prime example of this occurred when I studied innovative behavior amongst employees within a professional service firm. This firm had a very hierarchical organizational structure – which is not uncommon in these kinds of firms. In this case, a large number of employees were managed by a smaller group of firm partners.

My initial analysis showed that gender was an important predictor of innovative behavior. Men reported more innovative behaviors and were also more involved in innovation projects within the firm compared to women. This finding was in line with previous literature on gender differences.[36]

However, when I took a second look at the data, I noticed that most of the firm's partners were men. It turned out that they had the authority to come up with innovative ideas, promote these ideas and implement them within the organization. The women were overrepresented in the non-partner ranks. They had less autonomy to display those behaviors. Indeed, when I controlled for the employee's position within the firm the difference in gender completely disappeared. There was no gender difference between men and women in innovative behavior as the difference in innovative behavior could be fully explained by their differences in seniority/authority. This shows the importance having a second look at your data analysis and the importance of adjusting for context.

To interpret the results in the best possible way, you should have an intimate knowledge of what's going on in the business. This is very helpful for explaining the patterns in the data and for creating a plan to act on these findings.

Sometimes your findings will be hard to explain. Regarding employees, why are the number of hotel bookings, or the number of international flights predictive of turnover intentions? By talking to the employees themselves you will find that being away from home is taxing on relationships and that extensive travel involves stress. These effects will be more profound for specific demographics. A friend of mine told me that women in their early 30s in her firm are much more likely to leave the company when they have to travel a lot, especially if they were recently married. This was a profound problem in their firm's internationally operating division. In this specific firm the women in that age group often wanted to settle down and have kids – but their busy job interfered with this, so they quit. Talking to the people involved in the analysis will offer you a great deal of context that will help to explain your findings.

Presenting your findings

The final step is the presentation of your results. How will you sell your results to the business? Who is your audience? How will you distribute your message to them? Moreover, how will you explain your findings?

These are all the questions you need to answer before you present your results. We already discussed this in chapter five: you need to *sell* the results. The way you present and visualize your data is essential to effectively communicate your message. An HR dashboard with information for managers is usually ineffective because managers will forget about it – and thus not use it.[37] In this case, a monthly email with a nice looking report would serve your purpose better as this is easily opened and also acts as a reminder for the managers.

Depending on the organization, you can use different means to communicate your findings and message. Think about these ways and use them to your advantage as they are unique for every organization. A communication app like Slack offers easy app integration possibilities and enables you to seamlessly integrate tooling directly into the way people communicate with each other. A short, well timed message on this app can be more impactful than an entire HR dashboard. The take-home message is that you need to make the data as easily accessible as possible while keeping your message stupidly simple.

Another rule of thumb is to not present findings without (having at least thought about) a concrete follow-up plan of interventions that can help you solve the problem. For example, when turnover is too high, look for the factors that drive turnover and devise interventions that can solve the root of the problem. By focusing on the actionability of your analysis you will find that people are much more willing (and able) to act on your findings. The same mantra of the previous paragraph applies: keep it simple, stupid.

Lastly, you need to consider who you want to share your information with. It is common in attrition analysis to estimate the chance that an employee will leave. What you don't want to happen is that a manager, after seeing this information, goes up to an employee and asks him/her: "I see there's an 80% chance that you will leave the company within the next twelve months. Why?". To avoid situations like this, companies like Hewlett Packard extensively train a select group of managers before they give them this information.[38] Your data and insights can be very powerful so use them wisely.

Return on investment

One of the commonly heard arguments is that, if you want your findings to *really* have impact, you should relate them to the Holy Grail of people analytics: return on investment (ROI). Often, the reasoning behind this is that finding a financial number creates a clear and urgent message to directors and managers: investing in people efforts will earn us money. That's why a solid business case will greatly benefit the adoption of your findings. Managers will love it when you come up with an ROI.

However, a word of caution. Linking people policies to an ROI is very difficult to do and requires you to be very creative in your approach to build a business case, especially when you talk about softer concepts like engagement. An additional disadvantage is that an ROI often focuses on short-term gains: If a company can save money in the short-term, ROI will be higher. However, this does not mean that a higher ROI benefits the HR processes, builds towards a company's competitive advantage or improve organizational effectiveness. An ROI is not the Holy Grail: it is one of multiple factors that should influence decision-making.

There are easier alternatives to an ROI number. We already mentioned turnover: you can calculate the cost of employee turnover relatively easily. There are multiple tools available that help you do this. Any reduction in turnover will benefit your bottom-line performance and thus create a compelling story. We previously spoke about Credit Suisse (Chapter 2). They found that a one point reduction in turnover saved them 75 million to 100 million U.S. dollars a year! This is a compelling story. The same can be done for absentee-ism as these costs are also relatively easy to quantify.

Rinse and repeat[39]

Now that you've finished the last five chapters of this book, you've probably gained enough insights to think data-driven and go back to your analytics cycle, and repeat it. The fun of people analytics is that you make better decisions by analyzing your data in a smarter way.

This goes both ways. By looking more closely you'll find details which influence how people behave and react, like how someone's seniority influences their innovative behavior. Yet by taking a step back and looking at the broader picture, you'll discover different factors at a higher level that may have influenced your findings; like a new CEO who set a new strategy or recent budget cuts that had an impact on people's behavior and attitudes.

Unfortunately, not all HR analytics projects will succeed. Some never really get off the ground and others don't produce tangible results. To wrap this book up, I will briefly discuss five reasons (in no particular order) why HR analytics projects fail. This list adds a lot of value as it goes into the most common traps in people analytics and thus it will help you to become more successful in your up and coming HR analytics projects.

Five reasons HR analytics projects fail

1. The project is too ambitious

It's easy to get excited when you start an HR analytics project – but don't fall in the trap of becoming overexcited. A grand vision and high ambitions are required to get HR analytics off the ground, but they should not apply to the first few projects. Often companies bite off more than they can chew and end up getting stuck in projects that are too large to manage. These projects can take years before they're completed, cost tremendous amounts of money and produce results that are no longer relevant.

Especially early on, the HR analytics project leader should plan for and *create* short-term wins. These short-term wins are the simplest and quickest kind of analysis, requiring the least amount of data but adding the best value to the company.

"Here's that quiet little project we've been doing in HR."

These wins are very important. They enable the team to learn and work together more effectively, while increasing the visibility of the HR analytics project throughout the organization. As some people tend to be skeptical about HR analytics, it's important to demonstrate its value early on in the project by presenting these short-term wins.

The development of analytical competencies and increased visibility are pivotal in establishing HR analytics as a competency center within the organization and therefore reinforces the importance of short-term wins. A side effect is that it will also increase interest from middle and senior management throughout the company. In turn, this will expedite the implementation of the project's outcomes.[40]

2. Lack of relevance to the business

A second trap, which may be just as common as the first one, is a lack of relevance to the business. It's not uncommon for an analytics project to focus on an interesting topic which doesn't actually add value to the business.

Attrition analytics is one of the most talked about examples of HR analytics and is a starting point for many HR analytics projects. However, when attrition is not a core business problem, the results of the analysis do not add value to the business.

A good rule of thumb is to focus on one of the top 3 business priorities of the CEO. The CEO is not concerned about the number of employees he has or about the latest engagement scores. He's concerned about whether he has the right people with the right skills to execute the company's strategy, and he wants to know how he can increase his revenue while minimizing costs.

Only by focusing on a top business priority will HR analytics provide tangible value.

3. Compliance was not factored in from the beginning

Compliancy is becoming increasingly important. The HR analytics project has to be tailored based on both the internal company policies and the external, (trans)national regulations. Industries like banks and hospitals have strict internal policies on how data should and should not be exchanged and/or analyzed. In addition, national and European laws on data handling are becoming ever more stringent (e.g., the Reform of EU data protection rules and the EU-U.S. Privacy Shield are recent examples).[41] [42]

It's not uncommon for HR to discover that they cannot gain access to email or social network data, or fail to gain access to individual employee survey data because the employees were promised full anonymity. Involving compliancy early in the project will increase the chances of a project's success, and prevent the investment of time and resources on projects that were doomed to fail from the start.

4. Bad data

A fourth reason why HR projects fail is bad and messy data. It's commonly known that HR data is not the most pristine: unlike finance, the numbers never need to add up perfectly. It's not rare for things like function or department names to be mislabeled or abbreviated in different ways. In addition, there are often messy records of promotions and previous functions within the same company, if at all, which makes it hard to track employment history.

Bad data can make a project fail in two major ways. Firstly, the analysis can become distorted when data is mislabeled; e.g., one job type could be analyzed as two different jobs due to a typo. As the saying goes "garbage in, garbage out" – which means that poor quality of input always produces erroneous output.

Secondly, cleaning the data is a very time-consuming process and can take months or even years. Bigger firms like multinationals sometimes use different software systems in different countries, and use different data (entry) procedures between those countries. Add cultural differences to the mix, on topics like performance, and you run the risk of comparing apples to oranges. Especially in these situations, it's exceptionally relevant to focus on smaller projects with short-term wins as they require less data cleaning.

5. No translation to actionable insights

Our final pitfall is a lack of translation to actionable insights. HR analytics may produce some very interesting findings about a top business problem. However, these insights hold no value when it's impossible to take action.

For example, it's very hard to change things like an employee's sex or age. These variables are interesting and should be included in an analysis as control variables, but they cannot easily be manipulated (i.e., you cannot change sex). Other attributes, like engagement, can be influenced through various interventions. It's therefore much more useful to see how engagement levels impact bottom line per-formance than to see how sex impacts turnover intentions.

Of course, it is *interesting* to know how sex impacts turnover inten-tions, but you cannot act on this insight. What is interesting is WHY sex would impact one's turnover intentions – and of course what you can do to influence these reasons. Focusing on the actionability of your data and outcomes is important in order to come up with solutions that people can work with and implement to make better people decisions.

HR analytics is still a novel approach for a lot of companies and its projects are therefore prone to fail. By focusing on top business priorities, by including compliancy early on and by planning quick wins, an HR analytics project can greatly improve its chance of success. The quick wins are crucial, because they force the project team to define a specific question whose answer doesn't require huge amounts of data (cleaning), yet also boosts the team's morale and visibility within the organization.

CONCLUSION

This book describes the basic principles of people analytics. My aim for this book was to convince you, the reader, that working in a more data-driven way offers great value to both the Human Resource department and the company as a whole. Moreover, making decisions in a more data-driven way increases the potential of having better business outcomes.

The application of data-driven decision making to people management is still in its infancy, but its growing rapidly. I hope this book showed you that traditional human decision-making and people analytics are not opposites. When used correctly, people analytics can supplement human decision-making in a unique way by providing the insights necessary to make better decisions and achieve better outcomes. My aim was to inspire you to advance people analytics within your company and to take data management seriously.

This is also what we strive to do at AnalyticsinHR.com.

On the back of our business cards there is a quote by William Edwards Deming. Deming was a famous American mathematician and statistician who helped spur the Japanese post-war economic miracle of the 1950s and 1960s whereby Japan rose to have the world's second largest economy. Renowned for his work on the plan-do-check-act iterative management method, which formed the basis of the lean manufacturing method, Deming famously said:

"Without data you're just another person with an opinion"

Erik van Vulpen

REFERENCES

[1] To read more about how Google manages people using data, check Bock, L. (2015). *Work rules!: Insights from inside Google that will transform how you live and lead* (First edition.). New York: Twelve.

[2] Quartz (2013, May 1). *Bloomberg's culture is all about omniscience, down to the last keystroke.* Retrieved from http://qz.com/83862/bloomberg-culture-is-all-about-omniscience-down-to-the-last-keystroke/

[3] Business Insider (2013, March 15). *Companies Are Putting Sensors On Employees To Track Their Every Move.* Retrieved from http://www.businessinsider.com.au/tracking-employees-with-productivity-sensors-2013-3

[4] The Saylor Foundation (2013). *Scientific Management Theory and the Ford Motor Company.* Retrieved from https://www.saylor.org/site/wp-content/uploads/2013/08/Saylor.orgs-Scientific-Management-Theory-and-the-Ford-Motor-Company.pdf

[5] EyeWitness to History (2005). *Henry Ford Changes the World, 1908.* Retrieved from http://www.eyewitnesstohistory.com/ford.htm.

[6] Meyer (1981). *The Five Dollar Day: Labor Management and Social Control in the Ford Motor Company, 1908-1921.* SUNY Press, New York.

[7] Willamette University, *SOPHISTICATION OF MASS PRODUCTION.* Retrieved from http://www.willamette.edu/~fthompso/MgmtCon/Scientific_Management.html.

[8] Chimoga (2014). *THE EVOLUTION OF HUMAN RESOURCE MANAGEMENT.* Retrieved from https://www.academia.edu/6814032/THE_EVOLUTION_OF_HUMAN_RESOURCE_MANAGEMENT_Introduction.

[9] Grant (2010). *Human Relations Management Theory Key Terms.* Retrieved from http://www.business.com/management-theory/human-relations-management-theory-key-terms/

[10] Lievens (2011). *Human Resource Management. Back to Basics* (7th). LannooCampus, Leuven.

[11] Sundmark (2016). *People Analytics – An Example Using R.* Retrieved from https://www.linkedin.com/pulse/people-analytics-example-using-r-lyndon-sundmark

[12] Heuvel & Bondarouk (2016). *The Rise (and Fall) of HR Analytics: A Study into the Future Applications, Value, Structure, and System Support.* Retrieved from http://doc.utwente.nl/99593/1/Van%20den%20Heuvel%20Bondarouk%202016%20HRIC%20Sidney%20-%20Metis.pdf

[13] Examples from Eric Siegel's book Predictive Analytics (2013). Eric Siegel (2013). *Predictive Analytics: The Power to Predict Who Will Click, Buy, Lie or Die.* John Wiley & Sons, Inc.

[14] LA Times (2008, June 23). *The prince of hunger.* Retrieved from http://articles.latimes.com/2008/jun/23/opinion/ed-food23

[15] KARP Resources, ICIC (2014). *Estimated Food Spending at Hospital Anchors in Baltimore.* Retrieved from https://c.ymcdn.com/sites/www.abagrantmakers.org/resource/resmgr/BIP/Hospital_Anchor_Addendum_8.2.pdf

[16] The Guardian (2004, July 12). *Muslim names harm job chances.* Retrieved from https://www.theguardian.com/money/2004/jul/12/discriminationatwork.workandcareers

[17] Steve McConnell (2011, January 9). *10x Software Development.* Retrieved from http://web.archive.org/web/20130327120705/http:/forums.construx.com:80/blogs/stevemcc/archive/2011/01/09/origins-of-10x-how-valid-is-the-underlying-research.aspx

[18] The war for talent was coined by Steven Hankin of McKinsey and Company. The topic is increasingly mentioned in the past few years.

[19] The best example is a study published in Science in which researches attempted to replicate a hundred experiments published in top journals in 2008. The researchers could only replicate one third to a half of these studies. Source: Open Science Collaboration, Nosek, Brian A., Aarts, Alexander A., Anderson, Christopher J., Anderson, Joanna E. and Kappes, Heather Barry, ... (2015) Estimating the reproducibility of psychological science. *Science, 349* (6251).

[20] Centraal Bureau voor de Statistiek (2014, June 30). *Ziekteverzuim oudere werknemer zonder aandoening vrijwel even hoog als van jongere.*

https://www.cbs.nl/nl-nl/nieuws/2014/27/ziekteverzuim-oudere-werknemer-zonder-aandoening-vrijwel-even-hoog-als-van-jongere [Dutch].

[21] Wayne Cascio and John Boudreau (2010). *Investing in people: Financial impact of human resource initiatives.* NJ, Ft Press.

[22] HayGroup (2013, June 5). *Nederland laagste personeelsverloop van Europa.* http://www.haygroup.com/nl/Press/Details.aspx?ID=37385 [Dutch].

[23] Rasmussen, T., & Ulrich, D. (2015). Learning from practice: how HR analytics avoids being a management fad. *Organizational Dynamics, 44*(3), 236-242. http://www.sciencedirect.com/science/article/pii/S0090261615000443.

[24] Oxford Economics commissioned by Unum (2014, February): "The Cost of Brain Drain". http://cdn2.hubspot.net/hubfs/234061/brain-drain-2.png?t=1445594426502.

[25] Karlun Borysenko (2015, April 22). *What Was Management Thinking? The High Cost Of Employee Turnover.* Retrieved from http://www.eremedia.com/tlnt/what-was-leadership-thinking-the-shockingly-high-cost-of-employee-turnover/.

[26] Economic Times India (2015, May 25). *A bad hire can cost 5 times his annual salary to a firm: Report.* Retrieved from http://articles.economictimes.indiatimes.com/2015-05-25/news/62624552_1_bad-hire-annual-salary-organisation.

[27] Linkedin (2014). Employees Overboard: why employees jump ship and how much it's costing companies. Retrieved from https://content.linkedin.com/content/dam/business/talent-solutions/global/en_us/blog/2014/03/Internal-Mobility-LinkedIn.jpg.

[28] Ulrich, D., & Dulebohn, J. H. (2015). Are we there yet? What's next for HR? *Human Resource Management Review, 25*(2), 188-204. Retrieved from https://michiganross.umich.edu/sites/default/files/uploads/RTIA/pdfs/dulrich_wp_arewethereyet.pdf

[29] Thomasnet.com (2006, March 27). *Downtime Costs Auto Industry $22k/Minute – Survey.* Retrieved from http://news.thomasnet.com/companystory/downtime-costs-auto-industry-22k-minute-survey-481017.

[30] Groysberg, B., Nanda, A., & Nohria, N. (2004). The risky business of hiring stars. Harvard business review, 82(5), 92-101. Retrieved from https://hbr.org/2004/05/the-risky-business-of-hiring-stars

[31] For more information, check http://hockeyanalytics.com/2008/01/the-ten-laws-of-hockey-analytics/.

[32] Tim Harford (2014, March 28). *Big data: are we making a big mistake?* Retrieved from https://www.ft.com/content/21a6e7d8-b479-11e3-a09a-00144feabdc0#axzz32n17LQF9.

[33] Gartner (2016). Forecast Snapshot: Prescriptive Analytics, Worldwide, 2016. Retrieved from https://www.gartner.com/doc/3202617/forecast-snapshot-prescriptive-analytics-worldwide

[34] In scientific research, 'associated with' is generally used when people talk about correlations, and 'related to' is used when people talk about a predictive relationship.

[35] The official term is *line of least square*. The distance between the line and the individual data points is *squared* in order to achieve the best fit (by squaring this line, longer distances between the line and the points are penalized). The line with the least squares is the line that fits the model best.

[36] See for example Millward, L. J., & Freeman, H. (2002). Role expectations as constraints to innovation: The case of female managers. *Communication Research Journal, 14*(1), 93-109.

[37] David Creelman (2016). *Why you produce HR dashboards no one will use.* Retrieved from https://www.analyticsinhr.com/blog/produce-hr-dashboards-no-one-will-use/

[38] Eric Siegel (2013). *Predictive Analytics: The Power to Predict Who Will Click, Buy, Lie or Die.* John Wiley & Sons, Inc.

[39] Lather, rinse, repeat is an instruction often found on shampoo and has been coined the 'shampoo algorithm'. When taken literally, it would produce an endless loop that ends when the user runs out of shampoo. I wouldn't advise you to apply this principle in such an exhaustive manner on the people analytics cycle. However, do remember to always take a second look at your data.

[40] While writing this, I couldn't shake the thought that there are quite a few similarities between the implementation of HR analytics and the implementation of organizational change in general. The importance of quick wins are emphasized by Kotter (2007) in his famous HBR article "Why Transformational Efforts Fail". He states the importance of planning for short-term wins to create and keep up momentum. This is also true for HR's analytics projects, especially because the team must establish itself as

a functional team and position itself within the organization as a whole. Short-term wins are useful in achieving both.

[41] European Commission (2016). *Reform of EU data protection rules*. Retrieved from http://ec.europa.eu/justice/data-protection/reform/index_en.htm

[42] Buddle Finlay (2016). *EU-US Privacy Shield, Brexit - where to next for European data protection law?* Retrieved from http://www.lexology.com/library/detail.aspx?g=4f12c610-95c3-46af-ba47-405135081f86